Women's Right: Kids and Career

Praise for *Women's Right: Kids and Career*

"Our mom raised us on love, fun and a ton of structure. We did things we didn't want to do, like reading for two hours a day during the summer while our friends watched TV. Brutal, right? She demanded excellence and when we didn't deliver she asked why. Not the most comfortable conversations, but they made us who we are today…driven, passionate, resilient and reliable. She knew we could be better than we were able to imagine. She always told us we could do anything we wanted to do … a motto she not only preached but practiced."

Justin and Tara Goldsborough, my kids

"I managed some of IBM's best partners, distinguished engineers, and senior architects. I incorporated lessons that I learned from Cloene into my own management style. In 1998 I asked Cloene to speak at an internal IBM event. She mesmerized the audience. She is a gifted communicator who is as good as any I have ever seen. Cloene and I have a decades long relationship and I am proud to call her my friend."

Kim Krostue, Partner–IBM Global Services–Emeritus

"As a professional associate of Cloene's for over 30 years as well as a good friend I saw first-hand the successful navigation of her career in male dominated organizations as she broke through barriers to be at a peer level within the executive suite. Also as a good friend I became close to her family and watched as she ensured her children were afforded the best guidance to become successful adults. This book has real take-away advice that has immediate value to all women who want to achieve a meaningful balance between a demanding career and family. "

Sharon Butler Payne, Founder and Executive Director,
Bra Couture KC

"For many who want to have it all, balancing a personal life and professional career is an endless struggle. Cloene's book offers a real-life story that presents the challenges encountered and knowledge obtained while fulfilling one's dreams. From a "first person" experience, I know she has truly inspired many others' along the way. This complicated journey is so relatable. Brilliant, with a heartfelt thank you."

JoLinda Vega, CEO, JMV Professional Consulting

Praise for *Women's Right: Kids and Career*

"This book is a must read for women trying to navigate the difficulties of having a successful career AND happy, successful kids. Cloene's accounts of her journey through a male dominated business world and raising two amazing children proves you might not "have it all" but you sure can "have a lot!" I was lucky enough to witness her success doing both."

Brenda Davis, former Executive Assistant

"A key to success is having women that support each other as we're trying to build solid, fulfilling careers at the same time as nurturing and mentoring children through their busy lives. I had the privilege of having Cloene both as a leader as well as friend, supporting each other through difficult and trying times as well as high points. This book walks the reader through such journeys, and helps show you can "have a lot" of fulfillment and enjoyment along the way, and make lifelong friends in the process."

Cheryl Glidewell, former Director

"A must-read for all women looking for guidance on how to navigate workplace gender bias, achieve career success (even to the executive-level), and simultaneously achieve success as a mother—without the guilt!

"Cloene, a trailblazer for all working women, provides a roadmap for women's career success. Davis shares her unique insights, experiences, and practical advice for high-achieving and aspiring women everywhere. Davis covers everything from career advancement, child care, and finances, to the confidence factor for achieving success.

"Entertaining and practical—a great resource for all leaders and career women (with or without kids). A much-needed book whose time has come!"

Deborah Knight, CEO & Founder, Women's Executive Club

Praise for *Women's Right: Kids and Career*

"I met Cloene when she started at TWA and was pregnant with her first child. One of the many helpful things I learned from her came in handy when my kids were in grade school. I needed to figure out a summer schedule for them so I sought help first at their school. I was able to hire a young man who worked with their after school program. They had a busy and fun summer. She was fearless in our male dominated work environment and an inspiration for handling the challenges of raising children at the same time. I am so glad she has shared her experiences in this book!"

Judy Hispanski, former Senior Systems Analyst,

"Cloene knows how to juggle work and home because she's lived it. This book is a great thesis on how to navigate the challenges and opportunities of building career and family based on lessons learned from real life experiences."

Greg Goldsborough, Stepson

"Cloene is a trailblazer who with fierce determination sought career advancement and a meaningful personal life. She welcomed her stepchildren as part of her extended family."

Brad Goldsborough, Stepson

Women's Right: Kids and Career
... the Art of
Juggling Career and Family

Cloene Davis

with Brook Deaver, CFP®, MBA

Cloene Davis Press
Blue Springs, Missouri

Dedication

To my parents, Clarence and Foye Biggs. They set high expectations and loved me unconditionally whether I succeeded or failed. But there was no doubt they expected success. My dad encouraged outrageous self-confidence and believed I would soar. My mom made sure I could perform the practical things and grounded me in reality. They taught me the importance of family and friends.

To my brother and his wife, Jim and Sharla Biggs, and their five wonderful children—Lynn, Vicki, Denisa, Bruce and Missy. They were married almost 63 years before Sharla died in the spring of 2017. They were always there for me and provided a hideaway a few times when life overwhelmed me. I would go and spend time with their extraordinary family and get renewed. I would not be the person I am today without their love, support and tolerance.

To my children, Justin and Tara Goldsborough. The role of their mom is my greatest passion and their love sustains me. I honed the lessons in this book raising them.

To my stepchildren, Greg Goldsborough, Brad Goldsborough and Carrie Davis Wilke. They had wonderful moms so we are good friends.

CONTENTS

Foreword...x

Preface xi

Acknowledgments.. xiv

The Power of Passion 1

Part 1—My Life and Career 3

   My Early Childhood..4

   School Days 11

   College Life..14

   Adventures at Work..18

Part 2—Life Lessons for Managing Family.....................29

   Don't Wallow in Shame or Guilt! 30

   Resilience 35

   Learn to Outsource..38

   Learn to Say No...44

   "Three is a Real Mess!!" or Out of the Mouths of Babes!!.47

Part 3—Life Lessons for Managing Career 50

   Dealing with Gender Bias.......................................51

   Enhance Your Confidence 61

   My 51 Percent Rule...67

   Take Chances, Accept Risk 72

   Don't Make Yourself Indispensable 78

   Perseverance 82

   Where Did All the Administrative Assistants Go? 88

Part 4—Financial Planning..90

   When I Screw Up, I REALLY Screw Up..............................91

   What Cloene Could Have Done...95

Have the Confidence to Pursue your Passions 108

Appendix: Books I Highly Recommend 114

   Family...114

   Career 115

About Cloene Davis 117

FOREWORD

I remember the first time I saw Cloene. Her reputation as a smart and savvy IT executive preceded the actual viewing. Her powerful stance and confidence in how she conducted herself made me recognize why she was so polarizing, and fascinating. Although widely respected by corporate business units and her peers in the technology industry, she was a threat to the good old boys' network. Especially in the 1980's and 1990's. I think it energized her.

Not only was she a successful IT executive, but she was a wife and mother. As a young wife and mother and one of the few women programmers in a large corporation, I was a student of how she walked, talked, behaved, commanded a room and led high performing teams. I watched her integrate her children or talk about the love for her parents and not be embarrassed that she had a family. Rare, especially in the '80s when men did not want women to mention that they had family responsibilities.

In my career, and as an entrepreneur, I took away one of the best pieces of advice from her. She was somber when not long after following her to another corporation, there was a massive layoff. Her advice to our organization: "the best job security you have is making sure you are marketable." Cloene, you were a pioneer and an inspiration!

I want to recommend Cloene's book to anyone facing the challenges of juggling career and family.

Jeanette Prenger,
President and CEO, ECCO Select
December 2018

PREFACE

I wasn't thinking about starting a new career as a professional speaker. But then on September 24, 2013, I was asked to fill in for Miss Kansas.

I had just finished a consulting contract for a local bank. Before pursuing another contract, I decided to take some time off to deal with family matters. It's about 10:30 a.m. on September 24, when my mobile phone rings. It's one of my best friends, Sharon Payne. Sharon says, "Cloene, I need your help. There's this new women's organization called Women's Executive Club (WEC). They are having their kickoff meeting tonight and the scheduled speaker, the reigning Miss Kansas, just called and cancelled."

The president of the WEC had been calling everyone she knew to try to get someone and called Sharon to see if she could talk to the group. Sharon had another commitment but said that she knew someone who did public speaking and would call to see if I was available and willing. Sharon tells me, "I think this can be a great opportunity for you to kick off this new organization and help get it started." I did a double take and asked, "Did you say tonight?" Sharon replies, "Yes, it's tonight." I was in the car taking my husband to see his doctor. I told Sharon I would call her back in about ten minutes.

I called Sharon and she told me more about the event. They were expecting 100 women to attend. The scheduled speaker who cancelled was Miss Kansas 2013. When Sharon says this, I just start laughing. "I'm supposed to fill in for Miss Kansas!" I start telling Sharon all the reasons why I could not do this when she interrupts me and says, "Stop. This is ridiculous. You know you can do this. You have always said you could talk for 30 minutes without any preparation at all. You'll have a few hours to prepare. So just stop making excuses. It's just a 30 minute talk." I pause and ask myself what is the worst thing that can happen? Answer: I could make a fool of myself, but not likely. What is the upside? Answer: I could have a good time, meet some new people and leave them with some tips for managing their career and family. I decide the potential up-side definitely outweighed the risk of failure.

I stopped making excuses and asked Sharon, "What's next?" Sharon says she will call and have the WEC president get in touch with me. Five minutes later I get another phone call. Now it's 11a.m. and she has to be getting desperate. I tell her about my experience and some ideas I have for the talk given the demographic of the expected attendees. She tells me it sounds great and looks forward to meeting me that evening.

I get home around 1 p.m. and I have to be at Deer Creek Country Club, 45 minutes from my house, at 5 p.m. wearing cocktail attire. I do a bit of time management and determine, with all of the other things I have to do to get there by 5 p.m., I have 45 minutes to plan my talk. I start making notes for the introduction, the body and then the takeaways.

For the introduction I decided on "clever." In the spring of 1968, while I was a junior at Ouachita Baptist University, my dad called me on the phone. During the conversation, dad tells me, "Oh, by the way, the community is sponsoring a Miss Logan County pag-eant. It hasn't happened for a long time, but this year there will be a Miss Logan County and the winner will be entered into the Miss Arkansas pageant. I entered you in the pageant."

I said, "Oh Dad, you have to be kidding!" It had never occurred to me to enter a beauty pageant and I wanted no part of it. I was, and still am, an outspoken feminist and I had a very low opinion of beauty pageants. However, I adored my Dad and I was not good at telling him no. He really wanted me to do this. I reluctantly agreed.

I kicked off my talk by telling the audience "I am a substitute beauty pageant winner, Arkansas's 1968 Miss Logan County. Sorry, I didn't have enough time to find my crown and sash. They are in storage somewhere."

It was 5 p.m. when I walked into the Country Club and the first thing I saw was a life-size cutout of Miss Kansas advertising her as the speaker. Suddenly I realize that the attendees don't know Miss Kansas is not going to speak. The WEC president is gambling that

I will help her win the night. I walk over to her, introduce myself, and say, "I think I need a glass of wine." She smiles and says, "I don't blame you," and takes me over to the bar.

I don't mind saying that my "substitute beauty pageant winner" story brought the house down. It was an amazing evening. The crowd was energized, the chemistry was great. I got points for just showing up on such short notice. I am pretty good at extemporaneous talks, but this was one time I exceeded my expectations. It was a home run. I really connected with the audience. After I finished, some of the women in the audience came up to me and told me,

"I need to do something different. I'm really unhappy and need to do something different."

"After hearing you talk about 'the 51%,' I decided I needed to make a change and I will."

I found myself excited by an opportunity for a new phase of my professional career. I am passionate about helping women understand their power, their passions and how to be empowered. I am passionate about helping women find what is going to give them satisfaction, happiness, a sense of fulfillment, and how we can put it all together with our professional career and our family. After several speaking engagements, I realized I needed to write a book.

Writing this book is one of the most difficult endeavors I have ever undertaken. I love speaking to people and having a robust question and answer session. This lets me look people in the eye and interact with them. Writing is a lonely task where I spend a lot of time interacting with "myself" and I find that "myself" is never satisfied. I have never felt more vulnerable so I asked myself is this worth doing even if I fail. Time will tell. As with my speech to the Women's Executive Club, if the worst thing that happens is that you don't like this book, I can live with that. The idea of the potential for good is worth it.

ACKNOWLEDGMENTS

When I started thinking about writing this book I knew that I would need help. I immediately thought of Dick Titterington. I hired Dick as a Data Administrator when I was at TWA and he worked for me again at Sprint. He is a brilliant data administrator, a wonderful person and a published author. When I asked him to help he agreed. He interviewed me and did the first drafts of all the chapters. Without Dick's help this book would not exist. Thank you Dick!

I met Brenda Davis when she became my executive assistant at TWA in 1988. We became lifelong friends. After I accepted a job at Sprint in 1992, I again convinced Brenda to be my executive assistant. I have been lucky enough to have two fantastic assistants in my career. Brenda is one of them. She has served as the editor of this book. Thank you Brenda!

I met Sharon Butler Payne when she joined my team at TWA as a technical recruiter. Sharon helped me staff high performing teams at TWA, Sprint, Sprint PCS and Excelacom. We became lifelong friends. She changed my life when she called and talked me into accepting a last minute speaking opportunity for the Women's Executive Club (WEC). Thank you Sharon!

This book has not been easy for me. I am not a natural author … I am a talker. Writing this has made me reflect on my life and the many people who have inspired and supported me.

- Professor Dr. Bob Riley
- Professor Jim Ranchino
- Rabbi Zeke Palnick and Irene Palnick
- Mentor and Boss Dick Heath
- Mentor Ed Lassieur
- Boss Hardy North
- Mentor and Boss James Newkirk
- Mentor and Boss Paul Hessinger

- Boss Ron Ponder
- Boss George Fucui
- Boss Sherry Brown—the only woman boss in my career
- Boss Majid Naderkhani
- Executive Assistant Brenda Davis
- Executive Assistant Maraion Douglas

Colleagues and friends … If I tried to list all of these who have lifted me along this journey, I would inadvertently forget someone. You know who you are and I love and appreciate you.

THE POWER OF PASSION

I cannot remember a time when I didn't want to have children and a career. It was always clear to me. Perhaps because my mom had a full-time job. My mom went back to work when I was six weeks old. Her employer actually paid for a babysitter.

I have had a successful business career, rising to the level of Vice President at both Sprint and Disney and working as an account executive for major consulting projects at telecommunication companies in Canada, Germany and the USA. At the same time, my ex-husband and I raised two wonderful children who are working hard to follow their own passions. It is complicated but possible to have a career and a family.

But, and it's a big but, you can't harness the power of passion unless you clearly understand what you want. This book is a guide for developing a clear understanding of your passions. To put it another way, you have to decide what's really important in your life. Establish your priorities, develop a plan and execute the plan. This is how you find the time to devote to your family, your career and yourself.

I find it interesting how often professional women in the work place, who are very good at planning and executing, don't use those same skills when it comes to managing their family. Yes, I said managing your family. I know some of you are thinking, "Family is different. Managing my family sounds too impersonal. I could never do that." I was the family manager. I didn't do everything myself but I made sure everything got done. If you want a career and a family, time is your most precious resource. You need to be effective and efficient in your use of time. Effective means doing the right things—learn to do only the things that ONLY you can do. Efficient is doing the right things right.

If there's one thing women know how to do, it's putting together a plan and then executing that plan. I have been in your shoes, and that's what I did. I've had a lot of successes, made some mistakes and learned a lot of lessons along the way.

I am passionate about helping women understand how to be empowered and insist on their rights. I want to encourage professional women who want to have children to go ahead and have those children.

I am passionate about helping women find what is going to give them satisfaction, happiness and a sense of fulfillment. You can have both a professional career and a family. I will help you get there. That's what this book is about.

But first, I want to tell you a little bit about growing up in a small town in northwestern Arkansas. Who I am today is a direct result of the possibilities I learned from my family.

PART 1—MY LIFE AND CAREER

My Early Childhood

School Days

College Life

Adventures at Work

My Early Childhood

I remember the night I was born. It was May 22, 1947. Daddy dropped Mom off at Booneville Hospital on the way to my brother's dance recital. He was all boy and a pretty good tap dancer. I never quite understood how Mom and Dad got him to take tap dance lessons from Mrs. Donavan, the town music teacher. Clarence Jr. was all boy. He spent his time fishing, swimming, hunting with Pa, playing football, reading, and tap dancing. The word from the city librarian was he read every book in the Booneville Public Library by the time he graduated high school. His name is James Clarence Biggs Jr. and he was very important the night I was born. He named me.

A few hours after the dance recital, the doctor pulled me out. I cried once and then there was silence. I was turning blue so the doctor threw me from a tub of cold water to a tub of warm water and eventually I started breathing. Dad heard the one cry and then nothing. Of course, he was not in the delivery room. As was the custom in 1947, he was in the waiting room and knew nothing except that one cry.

I don't really remember all of this, but it seems so real to me. The story was told to me so many times when I was growing up. I can see all of this in my mind's eye. Daddy made me feel the panic of every second as he waited for that second cry. My parents had waited a long time for me. They never practiced birth control and had given up having another child. I always knew I was a cherished little girl.

Later the night I was born, my brother won the "name game." My mom wanted to name me Rebecca Ann and call me Becky Ann. In my opinion, that is about the worst idea for my name I can imagine. My dear, precious, most intelligent brother insisted they name me Foye Cloene, after my mother, and call me Cloene. What girl in the South in the 50's, 60's, and 70's would have ever been taken seriously if her name was Becky Ann? I was going to grow up and be a feminist, a civil rights advocate, outspoken against the Vietnam War, and a converted Jew. No way was I a Becky Ann!

Mrs. "D", my Mom's boss, gave my mother a baby present when she was pregnant with my brother. In the card she wrote: If it is a boy, name him James Clarence Biggs, Jr. If it is a girl, name her Foye Cloene Biggs, after my mom. Clarence Jr. had heard this story many times and insisted on Foye Cloene. Thank you Brother!!

If you Google "Cloene" you will not find many hits. In my experience, 90% of people mispronounce Cloene the first time they hear it. Once they get it right, they remember you. A unique and interesting name implies a unique and interesting person. Not a bad first impression. Parents should remember this.

My parents worked and lived at the Arkansas State Tuberculosis Sanatorium, but everyone just called it the "San". The San was located two miles from Booneville, Arkansas, a small town of less than 2,000 residents when I was growing up. The First Baptist Church and our school were in Booneville. Booneville is located approximately 30 miles from Fort Smith, Arkansas, which is located on the Arkansas/Oklahoma border. Fort Smith is approximately 50 miles from Fayetteville, Arkansas, home of the University of Arkansas. Fort Smith was the city where we would go to shop and the University of Arkansas was where the Razorbacks played Southwest Conference football. What more did you need?

Booneville is also approximately 30 miles from Blue Mountain Lake where my Daddy and his friend went fishing in their bass boat after work four or five days a week. The other important place was my Mom's family farm where my Grandma and Pa lived on their 80 acres. It was about one mile from our duplex. This is pretty much the essential geography of where I grew up.

***

James Clarence Biggs was born in 1910, in Oklahoma. My dad was the youngest of eight boys. His parents were James Samuel and Sudie May Biggs. They were Southern Baptists who owned a lot of land, a nice house, a saw mill, a finishing mill, forty houses for the workers, and a mercantile store which made them relatively wealthy and influential for their time. Daddy grew up the son of a prominent lan owner and businessman.

The local school only went through the 8th grade. It was too far to the nearest high school, so Daddy went to the 8th grade three times to keep learning. Family folklore says Daddy was wild, a ladies man and a bit of a scoundrel. In other words, he was the spoiled baby of the family. He was the youngest of eight boys. He was always a spiffy dresser… and a great dad.

***

Mom was born October 28, 1915. Foye Geneva Wall was the oldest child of Maude Amelia Porter Wall and Price Wall. The Porters and the Walls were prominent families in the Mixon Valley in Logan County, Arkansas There were cousins, cousins and more cousins.

My grandfather "Pa" was one of four sons. His parents named each of their sons after a famous Confederate general: McCulloch, Marmaduke, Shelby and Price. Each son inherited 80 acres where they built a home and raised a family. This was and still is known in our family as "the farm."

Grandma and Pa were Southern Baptists. Grandma never smoked, never drank alcohol, never played cards, and never cussed that I remember. She was a "serious" Southern Baptist and not a lot of fun. She adored my brother and tolerated me. She thought I was spoiled rotten. Pa rolled his own cigarettes, kept moonshine in the barn, and only wore his false teeth when it was absolutely necessary. I adored my Pa and he adored me!

Both the Porters and the Walls attended the Mixon Baptist Church and managed the Mixon Cemetery. The kids rode the school bus to the Booneville public school. Mixon was country and Booneville was town.

Mom worked in the cotton fields, helped her mother cook to feed the itinerate workers, and helped take care of the new babies; first Vola, then Ruby and finally the boy, Dennis.

Mom had to go barefoot in the summertime and she hated it. She would sneak in and put on her Sunday shoes and Pa would catch her, whip her and make her take them off. I never had to go barefoot but Mom created a shoe monster. You should see my shoe closet! She would be proud.

Mom was a good student and wanted to be a math teacher. However, she had to quit school after the 10th grade and go to work to pay the taxes on the farm. It was the depression and Pa could not find work. They could grow their own food and make their own clothes but had very little money. Mom could work in the Canning Factory at the San and make enough money to pay the taxes. She saved the farm and made sure her sisters and brother could finish high school. Mom always said she was going to get her GED before I graduated from college. She eventually got her GED when I was in college.

***

As employees at the Arkansas State Tuberculosis Sanatorium, my parents received room and board as part of their compensation. It was growing up at the San where I learned how to be self-reliant.

Located about two miles south of Booneville in Logan County, the San was the relocation center for all white Arkansans with tuberculosis. It was known worldwide for its tuberculosis treatment and for being one of the most modern and successful facilities of the day. By the time the facility closed in 1973, over 70,000 patients, adults and children, had been treated. Before the Sanatorium, the mortality rate from the disease was 80 percent. The Sanatorium helped to reduce that rate to 10 percent.

Besides the actual hospital buildings, the facility had many structures including dormitories, staff entertainment buildings, a chapel, a laundry, water treatment plant and a volunteer fire department. The complex was self-sustaining, housing approximately

300 staff members at the height of its use. The total population of the San when I was growing up was greater than that of Booneville.

When I was growing up our home was a one-bedroom duplex with a tiny shower in what used to be a closet. But we were lucky because we had indoor plumbing. There were two double beds in the bedroom. Clarence Jr. slept with Daddy and I slept with Mom. I am not sure of the sleeping arrangement before I was born, but the lack of privacy may have contributed to the delay in my birth. We lived in this duplex until the summer of the year I turned 16. I shared a bed with my mom all those years.

There were two houses across the street from our duplex. One had been made into three apartments. Mr. and Mrs. Davis lived on the bottom floor. Violet and Claude Moore lived in one apartment on the second floor and Christine and Clifton Barrett lived in the other. Five of the six had been TB patients and had stayed on to work after their TB was under control. Mary and Ed Garner and their kids lived in the second house. They were cousins. Beverly was two years older than me and Tommy was a year younger. There were several other children but they weren't part of my daily life. In many ways the neighborhood was like having a huge extended family.

When Clarence Jr. was born, Mom didn't go back to work for two years. Her sister, Aunt Vola, had a baby girl the same year named Fredricka. Freddie and Clarence Jr. were raised together. Aunt Vola took care of Clarence Jr. when Mom went back to work.

The best story about Freddie and Clarence Jr. occurred one warm summer Saturday when they were five. They had gone to town with my Daddy and were walking around Main St. while Daddy was doing something. Clarence Jr. said to Freddie, "Let's get our pictures taken." They walked into Jones Photography and told Mrs. Jones their parents wanted their pictures taken. The story goes that she asked them if there were sure and they both solemnly said "yes." She sat them down and took a series of pictures. A few days later Mrs. Jones called my Mom and told her the pictures were ready. Mom said, "What pictures?" I can imagine the conversation

Mom had with Dad and then they went and picked up the pictures and paid for them. They were pretty darn cute and we still have those pictures. What did I learn from this story? Cute and precocious were prized attributes in my family and Daddy had a relaxed definition of babysitting.

The story I remember about myself happened when I was five. Daddy took me to town and I told him I wanted to go to the Five-and-Dime store. It was across the street from where Daddy was visiting with some friends. He told me to go ahead. I went over and walked around picking out several things and took my stash to the checkout. The clerk asked me if I had any money. I told her my Daddy was Clarence Biggs and to just put it on his bill. The amazing thing was that was exactly what she did! Small southern town economics.

I grew up with a working mom. Mom only stayed home a few weeks after I was born. The San wanted her to come back to work so bad that they hired and paid for a babysitter. She was a teenager and her dad worked at the San. My mom working was the difference between being middle class and being poor. She cleaned the apartment of her best friend and picked up coke bottles just so I could have music lessons.

When I was born, Arkansas state employees worked 6.5 days a week. Mom and Dad had Saturday afternoons off. Around the time I was five, they got a full day off and not long after, the State went to a mandated 40 hour work week. My babysitter had to work the same hours as my Mom.

My parents both worked in the Commons Building where the San's employees ate their meals. Daddy worked from about 4:30 a.m. until 1 p.m. Often after work, Daddy went to Blue Mountain Lake to fish with his buddy, Opal. Mom worked in the morning from 5:30 a.m. to 12:30 or 1 p.m., then had three hours off. She went back at 4 p.m. to work the dinner shift and got home between 5:30 and 6 p.m.

When I was two and a half years old, my brother, Clarence Jr., told his dance instructor, Mrs. Donavan, that I was ready to start taking singing and dance lessons. At first, Mrs. Donavan dismissed the idea because I was only two and a half. But Clarence Jr. was insistent. He was confident I was ready. So Mrs. Donavan spoke to my parents and they decided to send me to lessons. I was on stage for my first dance recital before I was three years old. My dancing career was not spectacular but I have been a singer all of my life. I was never shy on the stage.

School Days

Mrs. Jones was my first grade teacher. She went around the room the first day and asked everyone what they wanted to accomplish in school. I told her I wanted to be the valedictorian of the class. Because my brother was so much older I actually knew what valedictorian meant. Twelve years later, I was the class valedictorian.

By the time I was seven, Clarence Jr. had married and moved out of the duplex. During school, when my alarm clock went off at 6 a.m., I got out of bed, dressed myself and then walked about two blocks up the hill to eat breakfast in the San cafeteria. While I was there, Mom fixed my hair. After breakfast, I walked back down the hill to catch the school bus. After school, I usually spent time hanging out with friends and roaming around the neighborhood.

Daddy had a mild heart attack in the car when I was nine while driving home from Boonville. When it happened, he pulled to the side of the road, turned to me and said, "Cloene, you're going to have to help me slide over, and then you'll have to get behind the wheel and drive us home." This wasn't the first time I had "driven" the car. It was an automatic transmission and I was tall for my age. I had often sat behind the steering wheel and steered the car while Daddy worked the pedals. But this was the first time I was "on my own." We made it home ok. Daddy had a major heart attack a few months later and could not drive for six months. Since my Mom did not drive, I drove them where they needed to go. I was nine years old (almost ten) and a designated driver! I grew up fast.

Once we got a TV in 1956, my Dad became a dedicated watcher of the news—particularly CBS with Douglas Edwards and later Walter Cronkite. He encouraged me to watch and discuss current events with him. I particularly remember sitting with him in 1957 during the integration of Central High School in Little Rock. President Eisenhower called up the National Guard to ensure that the African American students were safe when they integrated the school. He told me that we did not use the "N word" and that seg-regation was wrong. It was a dangerous point of view in Booneville in 1957. It was our secret. By the time I was in high school, I was arguing for civil rights and equal rights on the school ground and getting threats from the older boys who fancied themselves as members of the White Citizen's Council. Not very scary threats, just loud, since they had known me all my life.

My junior year in high school (1964) I decided I wanted to go away to a summer program. I would have to find the program and apply for a scholarship since we couldn't afford the tuition. I ap-plied to a National Science Foundation summer program at Grin-nell College in Grinnell, Iowa. I was originally an alternate and had to wait on pins and needles until I was informed I had been ac-cepted for the program. This changed my life.

I took my first train ride from Booneville to Des Moines, Iowa, where I met up with some of the other students and we were bussed to the college. I was standing by myself feeling very alone when suddenly I heard someone say to me, in what I later found out was a Brooklyn accent, "Hi. My name is Lionel Cherry. Who are you?"

There were 40-plus kids from all over the country in the program that summer. It was the most diverse group of people I had ever met. There were Jews, Catholics, Protestants, Muslims, African-Americans, Indians, Whites from the East, North, West of the U.S. and one Southerner—me. I did not personally know any Jews, Af-rican-Americans, Indians, and only a few Catholics before that summer. I certainly didn't know anybody from Brooklyn.

I soon found out I had been assigned to share a room with one of the counselors. No one else had a room with a counselor. After a few days, the counselor told me the story. The summer before, some of the Southern attendees could not adjust to the integrated, diverse environment. They behaved so badly they were sent home. The school had decided not to accept Southerners the next summer. However, when an opening became available, they called one of my references and asked if they thought I could fit into this diverse en-vironment. They decided to take a chance.

Most of the kids were from cities and big high schools with diverse curriculums including advanced math and science classes. Most of them had already had physics, calculus and statistics. Made sense—this was a National Science Foundation summer program. My high school only offered physics and calculus during senior year so I hadn't had those classes. Since we worked in teams and helped each other, I found out I could hold my own.

I made some lifelong friends that summer and learned I was not easily intimidated. I discovered I enjoyed people from different backgrounds with different experiences. This was the greatest college prep experience possible.

I came back from that summer and finished my senior year. I was valedictorian of my class. I got accepted at Grinnell College, the University of Arkansas and Ouachita Baptist University. Ouachita had outstanding Political Science and History Departments and financial aid in the form of scholarships and work study. I decided to go there. The truth was I couldn't figure out how to go to Grinnell. We really couldn't afford the multiple long distance phone calls it would have taken to call Grinnell and seek help.

College Life

In the fall of 1965, I was very excited about college. I always knew that college was my path to the life I wanted. Thanks to a combination of scholarships, work study and student loans, I was able to go to Ouachita Baptist University which was located in Arkadelphia, Arkansas, 75 miles south of Little Rock. I decided to major in political science and history. I also joined the marching band. I played clarinet in high school and loved the camaraderie of band. It provided an immediate community.

In my freshman dorm, there were three girls to a room. The community toilet and showers were in the hall. Girls' curfew was 10 p.m. weekdays and 12 p.m. on the weekends. Boys did not have a curfew. The dress codes were very strict for girls. No jeans or slacks in class.

My first roommates were cousins from Mobile, Alabama. One of them asked me to go home with her over Thanksgiving break. I had never been to Alabama and I had never been away from home over Thanksgiving. We had a great time.

During the first year, I also met my lifelong friend, Arlyss Friddle. She was in the theater department. I was introduced to my first homosexuals from the theater department gang. I had band friends, theater friends, political science friends … Christians, gays, African-Americans, liberals, conservatives and, in 1967, several Jewish student friends. A strange potpourri of very interesting people who made a mark on my life.

When I returned to Ouachita in the fall of 1966, I became very involved in the political science department. Dr. Bob Riley, who later became Arkansas lieutenant governor, was the head of the department and Jim Ranchino was a professor and my advisor. They were both exciting, outstanding teachers and the 60's were interesting times. They were proponents of integration, civil rights, voting rights, equal rights and became opponents of the Vietnam War. It was a hot bed of progressive thinking right there at Ouachita Baptist University. I already supported these positions but didn't necessarily expect to be reinforced in my ideas at Ouachita. These professors became my mentors and friends.

In 1968, I became the co-editor of an underground newspaper published and distributed to the students. This newspaper was protesting the Vietnam War and also the conditions at school. We called out some teachers and administrators who we believed were incompetent and unfair, as well as rules we felt were antiquated such as the fact there were curfews for women and not for men. Those of us involved thought we were very clever, daring and righteous. It caused quite an uproar for its time at this small Baptist campus. Compared to what was going on at a Berkley or on many other college campuses, it was lame. We would have been expelled if the administration could have proven who was involved. The administration was furious.

There was another consequential event around this same time at Ouachita. One day after my required religious class the professor asked me to stay. I had tremendous respect for this professor and really enjoyed his classes. He told me that he didn't think I was going to make it as a Southern Baptist and that he wanted to take me to meet the Reform Jewish Rabbi in Little Rock, Rabbi Zeke Palnick. After meeting Zeke and talking to him several times, I decided to take his Introduction to Reform Judaism class and, after a year of training, converted to Reform Judaism in early 1969. When I went home to tell my Southern Baptist parents I was converting, my mom started to cry. My dad looked at her and said, "Mother, we are not going to be sad. If this is what she has decided, it is ok." My hero forever.

While at Ouachita I worked hard and it paid off.

- I was selected as a representative to the 1968 Mock United Nations Program in New York City. Representatives from schools all over the country attended.

- I was selected in 1968 as one of two student coordinators for a community revitalization project in Mitchellville, Arkansas Mitchellville was a small community of black, misplaced farm workers. Dr. Bob Riley and Daisy Bates, an Arkansas civil rights activist, were the program sponsors. I assisted with the grant preparation and joined Daisy Bates in Washington, D.C., to present the grant request to Agriculture Secretary Orville Freeman. This project was funded by the US Department of Agriculture and I helped organize and manage the student activities in this revitalization project.

- I was accepted into graduate school at Georgetown University in Washington, D.C. I was stunned and excited but since it didn't include a scholarship, I couldn't figure out how to go. I should have showed up on their doorstep and pleaded for financial aid. **I wasn't bold enough! What if?**

After graduation, I joined a special summer program of OBU Volunteers in Service to America (VISTA). Professor Jim Ranchino was the director. I think we were paid about $35 per week. After a brief training program, I went to Little Rock and worked in a poor neighborhood organizing mothers on welfare to fight for their rights. I was shocked to find that in Arkansas a woman could not decide to have her tubes tied to prevent additional pregnancies. The law stipulated she had to have at least five living children and permission from her husband before she could have the surgery. Women would pay men to pretend they were their husbands so they could get permission for this surgery.

As VISTA volunteers, we lived in the communities where we worked. One day another volunteer and I were walking back to our rooms when a police car drove up. Two white officers got out of the car, stopped us and asked us what we were doing in that part of town. Being a privileged, white smart-aleck, I answered that this was the United States and we could go anywhere we wanted. They pulled their batons and told us to get into their car. We had no choice but to get in the back seat. They started telling us that this was no place for white women and we needed to leave the neighborhood or suffer the consequences. They were big and they were scary but it was broad daylight. After a few minutes, I noticed a crowd was gathering outside. People from the neighborhood who knew who we were just came out of their houses or businesses and quietly stood together. Pretty soon there were over 50 people from the neighborhood just standing on the sidewalk. The officers became uncomfortable and let us out of the car. As we got out, we asked for their names and badge numbers. It was my one life experience with police intimidation. In my white world, the police were the good guys.

One of our volunteers in a town in eastern Arkansas was beaten and hospitalized that summer because he was trying to integrate a lunch counter.

My participation in the Mitchellville, Arkansas, project and the summer VISTA program gave me experiences that shaped my attitudes for life. I was blessed with support from my family and community which gave me the confidence to succeed and the ability to have empathy for those less fortunate.

Adventures at Work

This is not an autobiography and I am not going to give you my resume. I am going to describe the work adventures that enhanced my career and success and led me to learn how to juggle many roles.

In 1969, I went on my first interview after I finished the summer VISTA program. I was looking at the want ads in the newspaper, which dates me, and found a job that looked interesting. I called and made an appointment with the owner. I went in for the interview, which I thought went well. The owner offered me the job and then he said, "You are the best candidate I have interviewed. If you were a man, I would offer you a salary of $7,200, but since you are a woman and will leave when you have children, I will offer you a salary of $6,000." With the arrogance and cockiness of youth, I told him he was breaking the law and I wouldn't work for him. He was genuinely shocked. He thought he had made me a hell of an offer. After all, $6,000 was a lot of money for a woman.

In 1972, I was working at the Little Rock Opportunities Industrialization Center, a privately funded occupational training program dedicated to the elimination of poverty, unemployment and illiteracy through education and vocational skills training. I met some wonderful people at this job who became lifelong friends. When it was time for me to move on, I decided to submit my resume to the Human Resources Office of the State of Arkansas.

A few days later, I got a call to see if I was interested in a job as a Budget Analyst in the Department of Finance. Without a second thought, I said yes. It truly never occurred to me that I had absolutely no education or training in bookkeeping, accounting, finance, etc. Those were the days! I had a degree and could learn anything.

The job interview took place on a Friday afternoon. I walked into the manager's office, introduced myself and gave him the referral sheet from Human Resources. Larry looked at the referral, looked at me and said, "I don't know why they sent you to see me. We don't hire women for this job." But this time they did hire a woman! The rest of this story is in the section on gender bias.

Soon after starting this job, I received an invitation to speak to the local Junior League. I still don't know how they got my name. They asked me to speak because I was the first woman budget analyst for the governor. I soon found out from my friends that this organization did not accept Jews in their membership. I never mentioned I was Jewish and showed up for the speech wearing a large Star of David necklace. The following year they invited the first Jewish woman to be a member. Barriers were falling.

While I was on vacation in 1973, I received a call from Vance Jones, Director of the Office of Governmental Efficiency. Vance asked if I could come to his office the next day. He wanted to talk to me about an opportunity. I was intrigued. When I got to his office, he told me the governor had decided to partner with IBM to create an Arkansas Information Systems Plan (ISP). The governor wanted me to be the ISP Program Coordinator.

I was speechless. This was the last thing I expected. I had just accepted a job working in the governor's Office as part of his staff. I was very excited about this opportunity. Vance told me I could have either job but he stressed that this ISP project was a very high priority for the governor. I would have the opportunity to work with the cabinet directors on the Information System Executive Committee (ISEC) and to provide regular briefings to the governor and to the Legislature. I accepted this job and it changed my life. If I had decided to take the job working in the governor's office, I probably would have gone to Washington D.C. when Governor Dale Bumpers was elected senator in 1975. I would have never met the man I married because he was the IBM lead on the project to develop an Information Systems Plan for Arkansas.

I moved to Kansas City in 1978, because my husband was transferred to the local IBM branch. Blue Cross and Blue Shield hired me to help them develop an Information Systems Plan. The project did not get funded by the BC/BS board and I was laid off. By the end of

1978, I was pregnant and I was beginning to worry I might not get a job until after the baby was born. Employers were not inclined to hire pregnant women.

When I was three months pregnant, I got a call from a local recruiter about a job at TWA. Their Information Technology (IT) organization was interested in adopting a new systems development methodology based on concepts of Information Engineering. I had received training and experience with this methodology at my Arkansas job. I interviewed at TWA with several people and within a few days they offered me the job.

My first job was Project Manager and I was assigned four people to be on my team. TWA had a history of layoffs and of moving good people around to save their jobs. That is how my team was assigned. Each of the four people on my team had all worked for TWA longer than I had been alive! Interesting dynamic! Not just a pregnant woman but a "kid" to boot.

Our mission was to select a Computer Aided Software Engineering (CASE) methodology to be used to enable data oriented/object oriented analysis and design of information systems. This was the newest technology designed to significantly improve the analysis and design phases of information systems development. The old techniques for analysis and design were not rigorous enough to lead to quality development of ever more complicated information systems. So simple. Just develop a plan to help analysts and programmers fundamentally change the way they were doing their jobs and eagerly adopt all of the new ideas being promoted by the industry. I was just about the most popular smart-ass around.

We had to develop a change management strategy which included finding some early adopters with a lot of chutzpah and help them succeed. This long term project gave me a lot of visibility with IT management and made them see me as a change agent.

In 1985, there was a major reorganization in the Information Systems department at TWA. James Newkirk was promoted to vice president and he promoted me to director. I was the first woman director in the Information Systems organization. I was responsible for data management. Data analysis and database design were critical to the success of the new development methodology (CASE).

In 1987, Texas Instruments introduced its Information Engineering Facility™ (IEF) to help customers create information systems and perform and manage business processes across their enterprises. TWA was shopping for a CASE tool and settled on the IEF.

The management team recognized that implementation of this new information systems development methodology would drive tremendous change management challenges through the organization. Newkirk decided to send me and another director to a series of change management classes so we could develop a successful change management strategy. Since this was a time when many companies were redoing core systems with this new technology, having change management as a core competency gave me another skill set that was in high demand.

In 1990 I decided to leave TWA after receiving an invitation from Paul Hessinger to join the consulting firm CTG. Paul wanted CTG to become the "go to" consulting company for using Information Engineering and tools like the IEF in developing information systems. His offer was directly a result of the skills I had learned in developing TWA's FFB system and as chair of the IEF Users Group. Once again, my core principle of embracing every chance to acquire new skills and improve existing skills paid off.

Before accepting the job, I made certain that my boss agreed to certain conditions. I needed to be home fifty percent of the time. I knew travelling was going to be part of the job, but I was not willing to be away from my family all the time. He agreed, and we made it work. But after a year, I realized that being home only half the time was not good enough. Mom was just gone too much. It didn't feel good to me and didn't feel good for Tara, my young daughter. So I spoke with Paul about this. Paul had lived up to his part of the bargain, but I decided I had to make a change. So I made a choice to take a job with less travel demands.

While considering an offer from Budget® Rent-A-Car in Chicago, I received a call from a local technology recruiter I knew very well.

This recruiter told me that Sprint had just hired their first ever chief information officer (CIO). It was Ron Ponder from Federal Express, and he was going to report to Ron Lemay, Sprint's chief operating officer (COO). Ponder was a great proponent of data management and was looking for someone to head up his data management organization at Sprint. This recruiter had told Ponder about me and had given him my resume. The recruiter asked me if I was interested in meeting with Ponder, and I said yes but Ponder had to know that I had another job offer. It was a whirlwind affair. I received the call on Friday scheduling an interview on Monday with Ron Ponder, had additional interviews on Tuesday and Wednesday and received a job offer on Friday.

The offer was for a senior director position in charge of Data Management and reporting directly to Ron Ponder. Knowing my family preferred to remain in Kansas City, I sent my regrets to Budget® and accepted Sprint's offer. It was a good job and was good for my family.

Ron Ponder left to take a position as CIO for AT&T. Ponder's leaving led to a reorganization where I was still in charge of Data Management and reported directly to George Fucui, president of Sprint's Network organization. I was still the only woman and the only senior director in the room.

***

One of the biggest opportunities of my professional career happened when I joined Sprint PCS (Sprint's mobile phone division) as the VP of information resource management. I finally made it to VP. Sprint had made the decision to enter the mobile phone market, and Sprint PCS was the result. I joined in the spring of 1996, during the initial systems build out for the new company. I had previously worked with the Sprint PCS chief operating officer (COO). The COO's vision was to build a comprehensive series of data warehouses. If Sprint PCS used the information stored in data warehouses to manage the business from the start, the business would find them invaluable and continue to fund them as the company grew.

I was asked to join Sprint PCS because of my data management experience. My team was responsible for building out the data warehouses that would be used to manage the business and to support database management for the numerous applications needed to support the business. We did implement the data warehouses envisioned by the COO. We started small in the beginning for a small amount of money and then scaled the platform as the business grew. The day PCS launched in two cities, the executives could see key store sales information on their new digital phones. The COO's belief that the business would find this data invaluable turned out to be correct. I distinctly remember the time I requested $33 million to support an equipment build out for the ever-growing data warehouses. Each department head I met with basically said, "Well, I can't live without the data warehouses, but I don't think anybody else is using them as effectively as I am." The budget request was approved. Nobody was willing to lose their "big data" analysis capability

Throughout my career, I have had four outstanding opportunities. The first one was getting the opportunity to be the program coordinator for the implementation of the Information Strategy Plan for the State of Arkansas. The second one was bringing the IEF into TWA and implementing a redesigned FFB system. The third one was implementing the data warehouses at Sprint PCS, which built the foundation on which Sprint PCS manages the business operations.

My fourth opportunity arose when Sprint PCS hired a new CIO, Sherry Brown, who asked me to be the VP of application development. This organization had about 1,200 people, more than five times the size of the information resource management organization. I was excited about this challenge.

A significant change was that I had 15 direct reports and we needed to make the organization a high-performing team. I thought our annual kickoff meeting would provide a good opportunity to show the organization how the leadership team could work together and I had a "great idea" for how to pull this off. I had attended my son's last basketball game of his senior year. The senior players did a choreographed dance to *Men in Black*. It drew tremendous applause …as much for their daring as for their skill. My idea was to hire the choreographer that trained the basketball players to work with us. I was so excited and then I mentioned my fabulous idea to the two women planning the event. They looked at me like I had lost my mind. No way would my direct reports, mostly men, agree to this idea.

I presented my idea at our next staff meeting and received dead silence! I explained that we would not look stupid because we would practice until we were good. Dead silence! Finally I said they would have to take my word that we would be a great success and their teams would love it. Trust me!

At the first practice, we were doing a turn and I got crossed up and fell on my rear. Everyone just stopped and stared and then I started laughing and that broke the tension. The staff could see that dancing was not natural for me and that I would be as vulnerable as I was asking them to be. The practices started in earnest.

One of my directors made an appointment and came to my office to privately inform me that he would not participate in the dance. He explained that he was just too uncomfortable and could not dance. I did my best to be persuasive but he persisted. Finally I said that he needed to remember I controlled his bonus. He looked at me as though I had lost my mind. I convinced him that I meant it and he finally agreed to cooperate. To this day I don't know if I would have really docked his bonus or not and neither did he.

The day of the All Hands Meeting we ran through the dance for a final rehearsal. I told them we were good and to just relax. But one of the guys who was the most hesitant in the beginning looked at me and said we needed to run through it one more time! The whole team agreed so we practiced one more time.

When the music started and we performed the routine the audience went crazy. They were on their feet clapping and shouting. We had to do an encore. We had worked hard, overcome our fear, supported each other and experienced a huge team success.

Two days later, the director I had to threaten to get him to participate came to my office and told me he showed his kids the tape of the performance and they were so proud of him. He had tears in his eyes when he thanked me for convincing him to participate. I loved leading this organization.

***

I left Sprint PCS in 2003 and worked for about a year as an executive consultant for Callidus Software helping the company market their software solutions to telecommunications companies. Subsequently an opportunity arose to work for one of the premier companies in America.

I received a phone call from a colleague who had been a consultant working at Sprint PCS. Now he was working for a project at The Walt Disney Company. They were going to launch a Disney mobile phone targeting families. The project was basically a small version of what we had done at Sprint PCS. They needed to choose a network provider and implement all of the systems necessary to run their mobile phone business.

They wanted me to join their team to roll out the Disney mobile phone. I accepted an offer from the VP of Technology to work for him as a contract consultant. The day before I started work, I flew to Los Angeles and had dinner with my new boss. I went to a meeting the next morning where he said he was going to introduce me to the executive team.

Imagine my surprise when I got to the meeting and everyone was there ... but my new boss. He never showed. Apparently, after our dinner together, he had gotten into a heated argument with his boss, gone back to his hotel, packed, cleaned out his office at Disney, and then left town. My new boss had quit, and here I am sitting in my first meeting for the Disney mobile phone project. Within a few days, I was asked to be the VP of Technology. This job required me to fly into LA Monday morning and back to KC Friday afternoon. I could manage this travel schedule because my daughter, Tara, was soon to graduate high school and was headed to Indiana University in the fall.

Once again I found myself working on an interesting and challenging opportunity. However, I soon discovered working for a California entertainment company was quite a bit different from working in the Midwest.

One of the first things I needed to do was to hire good people to be on my team. So I met with Disney's VP of Human Resources to understand the policies and procedures for hiring. After an hour or so, I said, "When do we do the drug test?" Well, everyone in the room started laughing. The HR VP said, not unkindly, "This is California. If we did a drug test, we would never be able to hire anybody." This was one of those eye-opening moments. TWA and Sprint were required by federal law to perform drug tests.

Something else I ran into in the hiring process had to do with compensation. Disney was accustomed to people wanting to work for "Disney" so they were able to pay less than going rates. They had no problem filling their positions. They thought it was going to work the same way with mobile phone technology jobs. I worked hard to explain to them that the skill sets needed to roll out a new mobile phone company were in high demand. The people with these skills know the market and know they are a scarce resource and can demand top dollar. These techies are less interested in who they work for than what they are working on. They are looking for the next best technology because that's what is interesting and what builds their résumé. It was a struggle but I was finally able to convince them that they were going to have to pay for technology talent.

I discovered another big difference in Disney when we went to New York to meet with Verizon to discuss using their mobile network. We actually stayed at the Trump Hotel. Disney had already talked with Sprint about using their mobile network but did not feel the Sprint mobile network met Disney quality standards. So I am sitting in this meeting and now understand what it means to be "in a room with two 800 pound gorillas."

Disney went into the meeting thinking Verizon needs Disney as a customer because "everybody wants Disney." The Verizon technology team was on the other side of the table thinking, "We don't need Disney."

At this point in time, Sprint was the only one who had successfully implemented another company utilizing their mobile network. That was Virgin Mobile. They knew how to meet the demands of a third party.

During the meeting, Disney was saying Verizon would have to create reports for them every day. Verizon replied that they didn't even produce reports every day for Verizon. Once a month or once every two weeks was good enough. I was chuckling to myself during this meeting.

At the next break, I took the Disney guys aside and said, "I am going to say something profound. Disney needs a mobile network. Verizon doesn't need Disney. Verizon would like to have you as a customer, but they don't need you. Everything will be a battle from day one. Their technology organizations will drag their feet. They just don't need you. They don't even want you because servicing you will complicate their lives. Verizon Marketing wants you, but not the technology groups that will have to make this work."

At the time, Verizon's mobile network was rated number one. Disney continued to negotiate with Verizon for several months. Then we started talks with T-Mobile and a few months after that we started negotiations with Nextel.

Everything seemed to be going great. We were going to use the Nextel network and their billing and business systems. This was also the time Nextel was negotiating a merger with Sprint, but we expected we would be able to conclude our deal before the merger decision.

On the night before Disney and Nextel executives were going to sign the contract to launch a Disney mobile phone, we were all together having a dinner celebration. The head Nextel guy got called out during dinner. Ten minutes passed and he came back and asked to speak privately with the head of our team. He tolf him that the merger agreement with Sprint was going to be signed tomorrow and Sprint didn't want to take on the Disney project. It was too much risk to try to implement the Disney-Nextel project and accomplish the Sprint-Nextel merger at the same time. Disney never did launch their family mobile phone. The window of opportunity had closed.

I spent the rest of my career as an account executive managing Information Technology consulting teams for telecommunication companies in Canada, USA and Germany. Justin was married and working in Kansas City and Tara was in college while I was working and traveling.

PART 2—LIFE LESSONS FOR MANAGING FAMILY

In preparing for that first speech to the Women's Executive Club, I created a list of 12 takeaways that formed the framework for my talk. During the process of writing this book I have read numerous books and articles about juggling parenting and career. I have listed these books in the Appendix so you can decide if you want to read some of them. After all that research, these are the same five life lessons for parenting I discussed in the first Women's Executive Club talk. This is real for me.

Don't Wallow in Shame or Guilt!

Resilience

Learn to Outsource

Learn to Say No

Three Is a Real Mess!!

Don't Wallow in Shame or Guilt!

> Shame is destructive. There is nothing positive about shame. Guilt is often a strong motivator for change. When I do things that are inconsistent with who I want to be I work on experiencing guilt as an opportunity for growth.

Brené Brown

A friend of mine, who is a professional career woman, once confided to me, "My son cried today when I left him at daycare, and I felt guilty for the rest of the day." Her stress level was sky high all day and she found it very difficult to focus on work.

I was certain her son had stopped crying after she left and tried to reassure her by saying, "I'll bet anything that 20 seconds after you walked out the door, your child was back to his normal self, playing with the other kids, laughing and having a good time."

I also tried to reassure her everything was fine. If her son had continued to cry and be inconsolable for an unreasonable period of time, Mom would have gotten a phone call. You have to trust the people you have selected to help you care for your children and you have to be sure you have instructed your daycare provider that they can call if they deem it necessary.

I've also known women who feel guilty when they do too much at home and feel it detracts from their job. They tell me, "I'm worried about not doing enough at work because I have to take care of my children." Or they feel guilty taking time away from work to stay home to take care of their sick child. Many women, rightfully so, believe they have to work harder than their male counterparts to be successful. Stress builds up because time spent taking care of their family is time they cannot spend on their career. It's a vicious cycle.

There is nothing women waste more time on than guilty. It's not only a waste of time; it's a waste of emotion. Guilty will drag you down, drain your energy, and drown you in misery. Learn to make the appropriate adjustments and then let go of the guilt.

Guilt can weigh heavily when you are trying the art of juggling between your family and your career. The quest for perfection at work AND at home is the enemy of good enough. The concept of "good enough" is very important since perfection is impossible.

Many women feel guilty when they do not live up to their own expectations of themselves and the expectations of others — mom, dad, sister, friend, society, etc. The most important thing you can do is to define what is good enough. This is a key part of managing your personal passions. If you find yourself feeling guilty about something, think it through and reaffirm you are making the best possible decisions.

When my son was three years old, he used to cry when I picked him up from day care. It was actually embarrassing, crying when being picked up! I asked him why he was crying. He told me, "I was having so much fun. I didn't want to leave my friends." I told him I understood but he was making me feel bad. We worked out a compromise. He could tell me that he wished he could stay because he was having so much fun and I would tell him I understood. He agreed not to cry.

Here is a list of some decisions I made and did not feel guilty about.

- Both times, I went back to work after a 6 week maternity leave.
- I nursed my son for 4 months and my daughter for 8 weeks.
- I did not pump.
- I tried a consulting job for one year when my daughter was five and my son was eleven. I was traveling 50% of the time.

After a year, as a family we agreed that even 50% was too much and I found another job.

- I accepted a job in Kansas City with Sprint instead of a higher paying, higher status job with Budget® Rental Car in Chicago. My family did not want to leave Kansas City.
- I did not participate in the traditional Parent's organization at my children's school. Their meetings were held around 8:30 in the morning. I had to be at work.
- I hired people to make homemade birthday cakes and cupcakes.
- I hired someone to clean my house once a week.
- Several times a week I bought healthy meals and brought them home instead of cooking. We tried very hard to eat dinner together as a family.
- Sometimes I would stay up past 10 p.m. talking to my son as he said, "Mommy, just one more thing." Even when I was exhausted. I learned that it is wise to let a little boy talk when he WANTED to talk. I treasure those late night conversations.

I was recently watching *Morning Joe* on MSNBC. They were discussing a recent study by Dr. Kathleen McGinn, a Harvard professor, which had been featured in an article, "Mounting Evidence of Advantages for Children of Working Mothers," by Clair Cain Miller in the *New York Times*. I have referenced an article discussing the results of this study.[1]

I was actually surprised when one of the very successful working women on the *Morning Joe* panel recounted a discussion she had with her daughter. Her daughter was generally supportive of her working mom but did say she missed not being picked up at school by mom like most other kids. The guilt and groaning expressed by

[1] Cain Miller, Claire. "Mounting Evidence of Advantages for Children of Working Mothers." *New York Times*, May 15, 2015. https://www.nytimes.com/2015/05/17/upshot/mounting-evidence-of-some-advantages-for-children-of-working-mothers.html?mcubz=3&_r=0.

all the women about how this was so hard and they felt so bad because they couldn't pick up their kids from school made me just shake my head. Guilt, stress, less joy!! This was a missed opportunity to help her preteen understand mom's decision to pursue a career and the advantages this brought versus the modest cost. These are conversations I would encourage moms to have and to give up the guilt. The world does not just revolve around our children. Opt for teaching resilience and joy.

When I looked more closely at Dr. McGinn's research, it occurred to me that I have reached similar conclusions through experience and intuition. I decided early on I could not work full-time and still do everything with my kids. I was not willing to give up being fulfilled as a career woman. So I decided to figure out which of my children's life events were most important to them and to me. I prioritized those events and figured out how to fit them into my schedule. I had the flexibility to work my schedule because I had a successful career and more control over my schedule. The more senior your position the more flexibility you have. I also talked to my kids so they understood why I couldn't do things like "pick them up after school." Because I was certain this was the optimal solution to accomplishing my personal passions to have a family and a rewarding career, I chose not to feel guilty about these decisions.

It turns out, based on this research by Dr. Kathleen McGinn, there is no basis for the guilt. Her research examined whether or not working moms had kids with worse outcomes than stay-at-home moms. Turns out daughters of working moms also tend to be working moms who earn more than daughters of stay-at-home moms. According to Dr. McGinn, working moms are great role models for both their daughters and sons, and "the role modeling effect … is so promising for women who have guilt about going to work. [It] suggests that you're really doing your kids a favor."

Dr. McGinn concludes: "Daughters of working moms see that it's okay; it's completely normal. That's what many women do. And it's okay not to spend all your time cleaning the house … Sons see something really different. Everybody has to pitch in. There's no good way to maintain a management of life outside of the home and a life at home unless everyone is working together ... Being raised by a working mom leads to much more egalitarian gender attitudes for adults."

So there's evidence you shouldn't feel ashamed about being a working mom and missing some of your kids' life events. You are teaching them life skills. They will be more resilient and have more grit. Don't feel guilty. You should be proud of yourself for being a good role model.

If you are following your personal passions, don't be ashamed about your decision to work from home or be a stay-at-home mom. There are positive and negative aspects to each of these decisions. Work to accentuate the positive and to mitigate the negative. Wallowing in shame or guilt only makes it harder for you to be in harmony with your decision.

Resilience

> Resilience can be learned; it is a critical skill for us and for our children. Resilience is the key to bouncing back from disappointment in order to thrive in life.

Cloene

Resilience is the process of successfully adapting to difficult or challenging life experiences. Resilient people overcome adversity, bounce back from setbacks, and can thrive under extreme, ongoing pressure without acting in dysfunctional or harmful ways. The most resilient people recover from traumatic experiences stronger, better and wiser.

From *The Resiliency Advantage* by Al Siebert PhD

In 1953, when I was six years old, I started the first grade. I caught the school bus with other kids at 8 a.m. and was at school and in class by 8:30 a.m. I was excited to start school and excited to ride the school bus. The second week, Becky, who was the eight-year-old daughter of the big boss where my parents worked, sat behind me on the bus and pulled my pony tail all the way home. I was crying by the time I got off the bus. No one would do anything because Becky's dad was the boss. This happened every day for the rest of the week. My brother was 15 and was on the bus, but didn't do anything to help because Becky's dad was the boss. He told me that I had to handle this situation myself.

The next Monday, I sat behind Becky and pulled her pony tail and she cried all the way home. No one on the bus said a word and no one tried to make me stop. My mom received a call from Becky's very angry mother that night who said Becky came home crying because I pulled her ponytail on the way home from school. My mom politely told her I had come home crying every day the previous week because Becky had pulled my ponytail all the way on the bus. The bus driver confirmed my story.

I was angry at my brother and at my mom and dad for not solving this problem for me. It was hard for me to understand that my parents and my brother were boxed in by circumstances. Then I was proud for deciding to solve this problem myself. This was little kid justice. Becky and I became good friends. I learned a valuable lesson very early on in life about standing up for myself and not expecting someone else to always take care of me. Years later, when I discussed this with my parents, I discovered t they were very proud of the way I handled this situation when they couldn't.

When I got home from school around 4 p.m., my mom was at work. She worked a split shift and went back to work from 3:30 p.m. to 5:30 p.m. I always wanted to call my mom when I got home, but she was not supposed to get personal calls unless it was an emergency. There was only one telephone in the Employee's Cafeteria where my mom worked. It was in her boss' office and the boss always answered the phone. The daily quandary—do I call or do I not call? It seemed very unfair to me that I couldn't call and talk to my mom for a few minutes when I got home from school. My mom had explained the rules to me and expected me to follow them. This is the only time I can remember really resenting my mom working. I am sure every kid of a working mom finds something to resent. Sometimes I would call and get grilled by her boss before I could talk to my mom. It was never pleasant because I never had an actual emergency. My sense of indignation was real and I am sure it was painful for my mom.

The important lesson for me was that I was not the center of everybody's universe. All rules did not get suspended because I didn't like them. I wrestled with this problem many days that first year of school and shed a few tears—maybe for 5-10 minutes—before I went outside to play with my friends. For a few minutes, life was tough, unfair, unreasonable and out of my control.

I finally learned to wait until my mom was home from work to share all of my news with her. This was an effective life lesson in patience and delayed gratification. I learned not to be a victim.

When I was a VP at Sprint and my kids had their first mobile phones, I had a similar rule. Don't call me at work unless it is important. If they did call, I would answer and quickly and decide if it was legitimate. The difference was I got to be the judge of what was important. My mom didn't have that power, but I did. I worked hard at school and at my career to be sure I had that power. I didn't get many calls from my kids because they knew my definition of what was important was pretty narrow.

As I look back over my life as a mom, as a career woman and now as a grandmother, I realize the resilience I learned from an early age has contributed to my happiness in all aspects of my life. We all know those people who go through life defeated—their glass is half empty. My glass is always at least half full and usually much fuller than that. Nothing is perfect and we all need to learn to live with some disappointment and challenges to rebound and appreciate the good times.

Learn to Outsource

> Learn to outsource. Spend your time and energy on the really important things, rely on family and friends for some, and hire others to do the rest.

Cloene

CAVEAT— I understand you can only implement parts of this outsourcing strategy if you have sufficient financial resources to "hire others to do the rest." Tragically, many women or families don't have this option, which makes their outsourcing choices more limited and more difficult.

One question I often get from other professional women is "How do you find the time to do all those things a mother is expected to do?" I know exactly what "things" they mean: making something for the school bake sale; picking the kids up from school; dropping the kids off at soccer practice; taking your daughter to dance lessons or your son to music lessons; attending dance recitals and band concerts; helping the kids with their homework. The list goes on and on.

In a subsequent chapter (Don't Make Yourself Indispensable), I discuss the need to empower your team through delegation. Delegation is also a powerful tool for managing the family side of your life. In other words, learn to outsource. Spend your time and energy on the really important things, rely on family and friends for some, and hire others to do the rest. This may be a financial sacrifice. We didn't have a big house or new, fancy cars. You don't have the resources or the time to do it all, so you need to prioritize what's most important for you to do.

When I was hired by TWA, I was three months pregnant. By the time I was five months pregnant, I knew exactly where my son was going to go after my six weeks maternity leave. Since I knew I was going back to work, I had arranged for daycare. I found the woman who took care of my son through friends and co-workers. I also knew where my son was going when he turned three years old. We were going to place him in Brookridge Day School, which was also recommended by a co-worker. Six years later my daughter went to the same daycare provider and then to Brookridge Day school.

I bet some of you are thinking, "I cannot trust a stranger to take care of my six-week-old baby." Believe me when I say you can find people and places that will love your children and care for them. I also believe you can usually tell when a child is not being treated correctly. No matter how young they are, you will know if it's working or not. They will be unhappy or fussy, and you will know something is wrong. You can also make surprise visits at different times to see what is going on with their caregiver. It's not just Mommy and Daddy or family who can love your children. Remember … it does take a village.

I like the title of family manager. Someone has to assume that responsibility. I kept the calendar. Maybe parents can share this role but I think that is very tricky. In our family, I filled this role. I found it easier.

When my son was three and a half years old, he performed in his first spring program at Brookridge Day School. They held the program in a big church, and it was full of people. There were 200-plus parents, grandparents, other family members and friends in the church. Just when the program started, I noticed my son walking around the auditorium with his class, trying not to cry. His lower lip was quivering and tears were beginning to well in his eyes. I turned to my husband and said, "I need to go up and help him." My husband counseled me to wait a bit. Seconds later, the head of the school, Judy Crawford, walked all the way from the back of the auditorium to where Justin was standing. She took him by the hand and they walked up the long aisle into the foyer.

I was sitting there squirming, wanting to go rescue my baby. I was trying to figure out what to do. About four minutes later (honestly it felt like an hour), I see this little boy wiping away his tears and walking down a very long aisle by himself. He gets back into his place and finishes the program and every program after that. Today he is a successful husband, father, businessman and public speaker.

I am not exactly sure what Judy said to him, but it was clear to me she loved him. She was a mom herself. She cared about him, cherished him and she convinced him he could join his class, finish the program, conquer his fear and succeed. He doesn't really remember this event but what this amazing educator did had a real impact on his life and on mine. She and a team of amazing educators were in his life from age three through the third grade. Today we really understand how very critical those early years are if children are to reach their full potential. There are remarkable people out there who can be part of your village and help you raise your children. You just have to do the research to find them and be willing and able to pay the bill.

You need to outsource those "must do" activities others can do as well or better than you because time is your most critical resource. Use your valuable time for those things precious: time for your children, time for your family, even time for yourself. I try not to spend time on things that don't meet my definition of important. For example, I have always hired a housekeeper. I learned about how great having a housekeeper was right after graduating from college. Great decision!

I am not all that interested in cooking. Don't get me wrong, I have cooked many meals. What was important was that my family had healthy meals whether I cooked them or not and we spent meal time together as often as possible. So when the school wanted cupcakes for the bake sale, my first choice was always to buy them. They were always homemade, just not by me.

Justin was four when he got chicken pox. He had about four or five actual pox on his body, no fever and felt fine. However, because he was contagious, he had to stay out of preschool for one week. His dad and I checked our calendars and it was going to be very difficult for us to cover work and stay home the entire week. This was before personal computers, smartphones, and working from home. I was trying to think of a good solution. I thought of my friend who was pregnant and had just taken leave from her job to await the birth. She knew Justin well. I hired her to stay with him. He had a great time and she had some extra money.

I always paid people to help me with my children except a few times when my mom came to KC to help. Sometimes they were friends and sometimes, people I would find, interview and hire. My son was five years old and decided he did not want to go to Brookridge in the summer because it was just too much fun to be in our neighborhood. I called around and found a college not too far from where we lived. I contacted them and said I wanted to hire a responsible young man to babysit my son for the summer. They sent a young man to be interviewed.

He was almost 19, had a car and was old enough to take the neighborhood kids to the pool. More important, he played soccer! He lived with us for three months and Justin had one of his best summers. His neighborhood friends had a great time too.

By the time my son was six, I knew I needed to find someone to pick him up after school and take him to his activities and bring him home. It wasn't important to me to go to all my kids' practices. It was important to attend as many games and performances as possible. I didn't miss very many.

I called a local public high school, Center High School, and asked them to recommend a junior or senior who needed a job and could help me with my children after school. They recommended someone, Joyce, and she helped us raise both kids. I did tell Justin that if for any reason this wasn't working out for him, we would find someone else. All he had to do was tell me it wasn't working. No questioning him about why. I told him he was in control.

Joyce did not work for us the whole time but was in and out of our lives for 15 years. She had two children of her own while she worked for me. My daughter was the flower girl at her wedding. She could bring her children with her to work. The arrangement worked well for both families. Joyce is still a friend and part of our lives. You can find people who can do the things you need done for your family, if only you are open to the idea. You have to understand what's important to you. Outsource those things you are comfortable with someone else doing.

I remember driving home from my job, getting more and more excited about what was going to be my time with the kids. My kids did not go to bed at 7 p.m. I would not have been able to spend enough time with them if they had gone to bed so early. So they went to bed between 8 p.m. and 9p.m. This was another decision I made to help me spend quality time with my children.

Their father and I chose to spend money on child care, private schools, housecleaning, and saved for their college fund. We started saving early for college. These were the financial decisions we made together as partners. Both our children graduated from college debt free because we chose to save money for their education. We chose to forgo doing some things for ourselves. This was a choice we made. It's what worked for us. Only you can decide what will work for you.

I was mentoring a young professional woman who was not planning on having children. She was a Harvard MBA and was working as the executive assistant for the President of Sprint. She thought she could not be a good mom and have a demanding career. During our chats, I learned she would like to have kids but had decided to forgo them. So I told her about outsourcing. She made changes in her life, ended up having twins, and is very successful as a mom and a businesswoman.

Learn to prioritize, learn to outsource, learn to delegate. By the time I was a director at TWA I realized it was impossible to complete everything on my to-do list. Every day I had to prioritize, delegate and outsource … at work and at home. I had to learn to do **what only I could do** and to delegate/outsource the rest. Spend your time and energy on the things that are essential for you to personally do—at work and at home. Learning to prioritize, delegate and outsource is really hard because you are being pulled in many different directions. I was grounded because I knew I was passionate about having a successful career and a family. Every decision had to serve those two passions.

Learn to Say No

> Your time is a precious resource. Invest wisely by learning how to say no when requests for your time detract from your personal passions.

Cloene

There are two limiting factors when trying to juggle between work and family. One is time and the other is money. Time is a limited, finite resource so you absolutely have to learn how to say no. In my experience, this was particularly true when my kids were younger because they took more of my time.

When I started working at Sprint, frequently working 50+ hours per week, my career began consuming more and more of my precious time. My reputation as a professional career woman was growing and I began receiving invitations to participate in women's organizations. I would have liked to actively participate in women's organizations such as Central Exchange and the Women's Foundation. I did attend some meetings, but I did not participate on boards. I would have liked to spend more time volunteering for charity. I contributed to the charities of my choice and went to fundraisers. Again, I didn't participate on their boards. It was a difficult decision when I declined these invitations but I just said no. I told myself there would be time later when my kids were older.

When Justin was in college and Tara in high school, I did join the board of Hope House. Hope House, an organization providing support for battered women and children, is an organization I supported for years and it was a joy to finally be on the Board. However, when I left Sprint to work as a consultant, my schedule included traveling out of town every week, usually leaving Sunday night or Monday morning and returning Thursday or Friday evening. I could not attend board meetings during the week and, after three years, had to resign from the board.

I did know several women who served on the boards of multiple organizations. With my schedule, I couldn't figure out how to find the time.

I had to learn how to say no, politely. **But before saying no to others, I had to say no to myself.** I had to decide what did not contribute to achieving my personal passions at the time. I could probably do it later, after my kids were older or if I had a job that was not so demanding, but I could not do it now.

Here are a few examples of the times I decided to say no …

- I never was a room mother at school. I always supported the room mother but I was never responsible for that role.

- I didn't have a home cooked dinner every night. At least two or three times a week I would bring dinner in—most of the time not fast food. We had some favorites that my kids loved. Olive Garden soup and salad and Jack Stack bar-b-que were two examples. Family has to have dinner; parents don't have to cook it.

- I always had someone clean my house, usually once a week. House has to be clean; parents don't have to clean it.

- I was sometimes a chaperon for temple and school activities or trips, but I was not the organizer.

- I quit a graduate program at UMKC after Justin was born. I was working at TWA which was 42 miles one way from our home. I made the decision to spend more time with my family.

- I was a supporter of Hope House which provides help for battered women and children. I bought a table for years at their All That Jazz fundraiser and made other contributions.

I didn't serve on their board until my daughter was in high school.

- I turned down a significant career opportunity at Sprint when the President of the technology division asked if I would be interested in being his executive assistant. This job was a career maker. It meant you were on a high potential track. I would have had to travel with him, help prepare for executive briefings and meetings across his organization. You really are completely at his beck and call for the year. Justin was in high school and Tara was in middle school. It was just the wrong time in my life to accept this position. This was the only career opportunity I ever turned down.

I learned to keep my "eye on the prize" which was achieving my personal passions for education, family, career. I wanted my children to have a quality education without debt. This was a primary passion. I learned to say no to a new car, a larger house, actively participating in multiple organizations, etc.

Justin graduated from Northwestern University and has a master degree in journalism. Tara graduated from the University of Indiana and has a bachelor degree in fine arts. Their college funds paid for these schools with enough left to make a down payment on their first house. They both tell me frequently how fortunate they are to have no college debt. They see how hard it is for their friends to pay off their college debt and buy a house. I had college debt and I know how hard it was for me.

"Three is a Real Mess!!" or Out of the Mouths of Babes!!

As a couple, my stepdaughter, Carrie, and her husband, Jeff, agreed on their personal passions. Carrie has a college degree and had a successful career she enjoyed. They knew they wanted children and agreed Carrie would be a stay-at-home mom. They have three great kids. One Saturday in March, 2014, Kate and Jeff were coming home from Kate's ice skating lesson. Usually the whole family went to watch Kate but this Saturday it was just the two of them. Kate was talking and said, "When I get married I am going to have two kids." Jeff asked her, "Why only two?" Kate said without hesitation, "Because three is a real mess!"

A few months later, Carrie was having one of those days all moms have occasionally. She told me that several of her friends were thinking about having a third child. Her advice to them was to wait until you have two under control before you add a third.

Carrie and Jeff adore their kids and they will be fine partly because they have a joint commitment to their personal passions. They understand the sacrifice of living on one income and the challenge Carrie faces day in and day out being home with the kids. I am very proud of them and thrilled to be a part of their support structure.

Maggie and my son, Justin, have a different version of their personal passions. Maggie is a graphic artist and after college had a successful corporate career. She then opened a retail store and grew her clientele. Their objective was for Maggie to work from home after they had children. Eric was born in 2012, and Maggie was able to close the store and freelance with as much work as she wants. They now have two kids. Betsy was born in January, 2015. This arrangement works for them. They agreed and are implementing their long-term plan. I am very proud of them and delighted I am part of their support system.

Tara moved to Los Angeles after college and is pursuing her career in the entertainment industry. When we drove from Kansas City to Los Angeles I marveled at her courage to relocate with no family and only a few friends. I am very proud of her and delighted I am part of her support system.

As I started doing research for my talks and for this book, I began to recognize patterns—preferences for having children two or three years apart, meaning multiple kids at a very dependent stage—diapers, needing to be feed, dressed, bathed, sick at the same time, multiple car seats, etc. The literature suggests that bringing a third child into the mix is frequently the tipping point for mom to drop out of the workforce. Three is a real mess! The one thing you can't change is the number of hours in the day and you do have to get some sleep. I want you to consider a different set of options such as having children four or five years apart instead of two or three. It is critical to understand every decision you make has consequences.

When Justin turned four and started his second year in preschool, he became noticeably more independent. He could feed and dress himself, entertain himself for longer periods of time, and play with others with less supervision. He moved from a toddler to a little boy. He had a life outside of home. After he turned four, we started occasionally talking about whether to have another child. We thought a long time about just having one child. Justin was 6½ years old and I was 38 when Tara was born. My brother was nine years older than me so I was not predisposed to having children close together. We were delighted to have a little girl. We never considered having a third child. We knew we didn't have enough hours in the day for another child. Enough love, but not enough time.

I loved having a baby and an older child. Since they weren't in middle school or high school at the same time we rarely had a conflict between their activities. When Justin left for college, Tara was in middle school. It was great having her home six more years. Justin had finished grad school before Tara started college.

We made these decisions partly based on my need to achieve my personal passion for a successful, meaningful career AND a family. I love my children and I really enjoy being a mom and now a grandmother. It is an essential part of who I am, just as being successful in the workplace is an essential part of who I am.

PART 3—LIFE LESSONS FOR MANAGING CAREER

In preparing for that first speech to the Women's Executive Club, I created a list of 12 takeaways that formed the framework for my talk. During the process of writing this book I have read numerous books and articles about juggling family and career. I have listed these books in the Appendix so you can decide if you want to read some of them. After all of that research, these are the same seven career lessons I discussed in that first Women's Executive Club talk. This is real for me.

Dealing with Gender Bias

Enhance Your Confidence

My 51 Percent Rule

Take Chances, Accept Risk

Don't Make Yourself Indispensable

Perseverance

Where Did All the Administrative Assistants Go?

Dealing with Gender Bias

I am an unapologetic feminist. Feminism is all about being treated equally, regardless of gender. In the workplace, this means equality of pay, opportunity, access, and influence. That's what feminism means to me. I have always approached my career and my life with this in mind.

Cloene

I have had to deal with some level of gender bias for much of my life. Sometimes it was very institutional and obvious. When I was in the third grade, some members of the high school girls' basketball team coached our peewee basketball team. High school girls' basketball was our only competitive sport for girls. By the time I was in the 6th grade, junior high and high school girls' basketball had been eliminated. It took Title IX to reinstate competitive girls' sports.

Most of the time the gender bias I encountered was subtle and insidious—like racism. I remember some teachers telling me that the boys would eventually catch up and make better grades than me, particularly in math and science.

Because of the blatant gender bias during my first job interview, I choose not to accept the job. I made this decision when the business owner told me I was the best candidate for the job but he wouldn't pay me what he would pay a man. I soon learned I wasn't going to be able to avoid gender bias. I learned to approach it head on, objectively and in a professional manner.

I am an unapologetic feminist. The term feminist got hijacked in the 1970's by extremists and this turned off many women. I certainly never burned my bra, quit wearing makeup or hated men! Feminism is all about being treated equally, regardless of gender. I was thrilled when I read the book, *Lean In: Women, Work, and the Will to Lead*, by Sheryl Sandberg. Sandberg, the COO of Facebook, tells her audience how important it is to embrace feminism. I believe everyone should be a feminist. Our fathers, our mothers, our brothers, our sisters, our partners, our sons, and our daughters should all believe in equality. In the workplace, this means equality of pay, opportunity, access, and influence. I have always approached my career and my life with this in mind.

I encountered another example of gender bias in the 8th grade. In school I had become a history fanatic. I wanted to take every history class offered by our high school. No matter how much I planned and re-planned, there were simply not enough time slots to take them all. So I came up with my ingenious solution. I would take World History in the 8th grade. However, there were a few problems. The high school World History class was a junior/senior class and was taught at the same time as the 8th grade Home Economics class. Home Economics was a required class for 8th grade girls. Ugh!

To support my argument, I put together a crude, manual spreadsheet showing when I would take all of the history classes offered in high school and that I had no time to take World History. I either had to take this class in the 8th grade or not at all. I showed my spreadsheet to my parents. Mom initially thought I needed to take Home Economics but finally agreed with my dad that we should meet with the school superintendent and see what he said.

My dad scheduled a meeting with the superintendent. He walked in and said that I had a proposal for his consideration. After I went through my spreadsheet and told him what I wanted to do, the superintendent did not even acknowledge me. He looked at my dad and said "Clarence, this is a 12th grade class. She will fail." My dad said, "Maybe, but even if she does she will learn from that failure." For some reason I never understood, the superintendent let my dad win the day. I like to think my spreadsheet helped but it was really the influence of my dad. I made an A in that 12th grade class.

***

It wasn't long after graduating from college when I ran into gender bias restricting my choices as a professional career woman. I have already recounted the story of my first job interview. Back then it was standard operating procedure to pay a woman significantly less than a man for the same job. I did not even bother to tell the owner that what he had just said was against the law. I knew the job wasn't for me and I left.

In 1973, I submitted an application to the state of Arkansas. I was selected to interview for the position of budget analyst in the governor's budget department that was part of the Department of Finance. Governor Dale Bumpers had reorganized state government by transforming around 50 departments into 13 super departments. One of these new departments was the Department of Finance. Each department had their own staff of budget analysts who created their department's budget. These budgets then came to the budget office in the Department of Finance where they were merged into a single budget for the state of Arkansas.

I went to my interview on a Friday. The first thing the hiring manager said to me as I walked through the door was, "I don't know why they brought you in for an interview because we would never hire a woman for this job." I actually thought "what the hell" but kept my cool and said, "Well, since I'm here, why don't we just talk." He agreed. I told him about myself, my education, and my work experience. As he listened, he started asking me some questions. When the interview was over, I thanked him for the opportunity to talk with him and left sure I was never going to hear from him again.

Then on Sunday morning at 9 a.m., the phone rang. It was the hiring manager. I didn't know it at the time but he had a big problem. One of his budget analysts had just resigned. This person just happened to be the budget analyst for the Department of Social and Rehabilitation Services, the state's largest department. What compounded the situation was they were in the middle of preparing the two-year budget for the state. Every two years there was an intense six-month period during which the individual department budgets were merged into a single two-year budget for the state. During this six-month budget cycle, the analysts worked at least 80 to 90 hours a week. He was desperate to fill the position.

I discovered the underlying reason he did not want to hire a woman was because of the work environment. All the other budget analysts were young men from accounting backgrounds, who were frequently insulting, vulgar, obscene, and used a lot of foul language.

He must have heard something he liked during my interview. I did not have a business or accounting degree, nor did I have any accounting work experience. But here it was Sunday morning and he was asking me to come back for a second interview. Of course I said yes and two hours later was in his office. It was during this interview that he described the work environment. He also asked me a lot of personal questions. I knew it was inappropriate and illegal to ask these kinds of questions but I decided to go along and answer them. The next day, he called and offered me the job. I was shocked. I accepted and started two weeks later.

I knew I needed to address the issues I had with the interview. So I wrote a private letter directly to this hiring manager, who was now my boss. I documented every law he had broken during my interview. I did not give a copy to anyone else. I took the letter into his office and told him, "This is just between you and me, but you need to know this." I then explained what was in the letter. I told him I wasn't angry and it wasn't personal. I was very professional about the whole thing.

I didn't realize it at the time but my manager freaked out about the letter. He had a close relationship with his boss, the director of the Department of Finance, who was a lawyer, and decided to share the letter with him. After reading the letter, the director asked him, "Is this accurate? Did you do these things during the interview?" My boss replied that the letter was accurate. After laughing, the director told him my assertions in the letter were correct and he should never, ever do anything like that again.

The next day, the director asked me to come to his office. We talked about the letter and my concerns. I assured him I had no intention of pursuing it any further. Then he told me he was putting me in charge of the new Equal Employment Opportunity Commission (EEOC) that he had to set up for the state. In addition to my budget analyst job, I was being "volunteered" to establish the process where hiring managers would be trained on the changes in interviewing and hiring practices that were mandated in the new laws supporting elimination of discrimination based on race, sex, etc. The EEOC would also be where employees could come for help if they felt they were the victims of discrimination. I considered this a great honor and an amazing opportunity. It was an important initiative and gave me visibility with department heads and the governor's team. This man who gave me this opportunity became a mentor and friend.

When I started work, I found myself thrown a third of the way into the fast and furious budget cycle. Until the budget was finalized, everything was recorded manually on paper—16-column accounting work sheets. I had never worked with these work sheets before. It wasn't rocket science; just basic add, subtract, multiply and divide. But as I mentioned before, the budget cycle was intense.

In the week leading up to my budget presentation, I remember leaving the office for a total of eight hours from Sunday to Thursday. I slept a few hours every night in my office. My presentation was scheduled for 9 p.m. in a basement room of the capitol with no windows. When I went into the meeting, the room was full of men. I was the only woman. There had never been a professional woman sitting at the table in these budget meetings. It was literally a smoke filled room. Governor Dale Bumpers was at the head of the table. It had been a long day for him and he was growing impatient. We were working on the budget for Social and Rehabilitative Services. In response to a statement by the department budget analyst, the governor exclaimed, "F---, that can't be true!" He realized what he had said, turned to me and apologized for his language.

Well, after about five times, I decided to speak up and said, "Governor, I am your budget analyst. You realize I play every day with the male budget analysts. You cannot possibly top what they say on a regular basis. You can't say anything I haven't heard or said. Why don't you just pretend I'm one of the boys?" The governor looked at me, laughed, and said, "Okay." We got down to business.

***

During my first week at work, I had to deal with another situation because I was the first female budget analyst. The budget analysts shared a staff of three assistants, all women. The senior assistant was a woman named, well let's call her Peggy Sue. She was about 45 years old and resented that I had one of the budget analyst jobs. One day my first week during lunch time, I was in my office working. I overheard Peggy Sue outside my door saying to the other assistants, "She took a job a man needs to take care of his family. There is absolutely no reason for her to have this job. If she thinks I'm going to do her work and support her, she's got another think coming. She can do her own typing. I am not doing anything for her." Since Peggy Sue knew I was in my office, I was certain this little speech was for my benefit. After listening to these sorts of comments for a couple of days, I knew I had to step in and put a stop to it. If the situation were to get out of control, I knew I would have a harder time dealing with it later. I preferred to handle it myself, without going to my boss. I wanted to give her a chance and keep her out of trouble, if possible.

The next day when the guys were all at lunch, I asked Peggy Sue to step into my office and I closed the door. I said to her, "You obviously know I can hear what you are saying. I have heard you say how our relationship is going to work. But I want you to understand that is not how it's going to work. You and I need to work this out before you get yourself and the other two assistants in trouble. You are going to work for me just like you work for the other budget analysts. You will type for me and you will do anything else for me that you do for them."

Peggy Sue was indignant at first and said, "You can do your own typing."

I replied to her that she would do my typing. Then I said, "I want to make myself perfectly clear. For now, this is just between you and me. It does not need to go any further. But if you do not support me like you do the other budget analysts, I will write you up, I will report you, and I will win. You need to decide how much you like this job. Following this conversation, the first time you fail to do something for me that you do for the other budget analysts, I will act."

Peggy Sue said, "It's just not right."

I replied, "Whether you think it is right or not, that's the way it is. I have this job. You will treat me and support me the way you do the male budget analysts."

Peggy Sue left our meeting angry, but she did decide to treat me like the other budget analysts. It took a while, but in another few weeks she came around and we worked effectively together.

There was another situation I remember dealing with in the office because I was a woman. As part of the office culture, the three female assistants brought food in every other Friday for the budget analysts. Shortly after I started work, they came to see me and asked what I was going to bring in on Friday. I said, "What do you mean, what am I going to bring in on Friday?"

They answered, "Well, all the girls bring in food on Fridays." My reply was simple, "I'm not one of the 'girls.'"

I asked them if any of the other budget analysts brought food. Of course, they didn't. So I wasn't going to bring food. Each time I was confronted with these situations, I decided what to do in an equitable and professional manner.

Once the state's budget was completed, most of my time was spent meeting with representatives in the Department of Social and Rehabilitation Services, learning about the business. It was an interesting and challenging job. I learned a lot about state government. I also learned first-hand about being the first woman to hold the job of budget analyst in the Arkansas Department of Finance. I had to learn how to perform my job responsibilities and how to handle "the boys." I had to make them understand they were going to treat me as a professional. But at the same time I had to make sure I wasn't too demanding or obnoxious or they would just freeze me out. Because of the way I handled myself, I earned a reputation of not taking every little slight and turning it into a "capital offense." I found that humor, instead of anger, went a long way. I walked a fine line every day and learned a lot about human nature and about working with the "boys." It was good training since I have spent most of my career with male peers and male bosses—me and the "boys."

***

After moving to Kansas City, I worked for Blue Cross and Blue Shield before interviewing with Trans World Airlines (TWA). As I mentioned in a previous chapter, I was three months pregnant when I interviewed for the job at TWA. I hit it off with the interviewing manager, Hardy North, and got the job offer. I had to go to their corporate doctor for a physical. When the doctor told me I had to have a chest x-ray, I explained I was pregnant and couldn't have an x-ray. By the time I got back to Hardy's office, which was across the street, the doctor had already reported the "problem". When I walked in, Hardy was both shocked and laughing. I asked if there was a problem. I told him I planned to return to work after six weeks of maternity leave. He did ask me what I would do if he withdrew the offer. I replied I would see a lawyer. He laughed and said I still had the job. I loved working for Hardy.

My first day at work, when I got on the elevator, there were two men talking about how Hardy North had hired a pregnant woman. One of those men was Hardy's boss and the director of my group. The director was shocked when I was introduced to him as a new employee later that morning. He recognized me from the elevator. I later realized it was a really big deal for them to hire a pregnant woman. They led me to believe that I was the first woman pregnant when hired. The law had just changed and pregnancy had to be treated as any other medical condition. Prior to this change, at TWA, when you left for maternity leave you had to actually resign from your job and the company did not have to hold your job. I had both my children while working at TWA.

I have also experienced more subtle but just as discriminating effects of gender bias in the workplace. In order to stay in Kansas City and not move my family, I accepted a job as a senior director with Sprint. I reported directly to Sprint's CIO. I was the only senior director on his team of direct reports. Everyone else was at least an assistant vice president (AVP) and a man. To this day, I believe if I had been a man, with my credentials, experience and accomplishments, I would have been offered an AVP position. But the offer was a senior director position for less compensation. This job did provide significant opportunities for professional growth and eventually led to my promotion to vice president at Sprint PCS.

One time a friend and colleague came to me and told me a story. She was a director reporting to a vice president at a technology company. I do not want to use her real name, so let's call her Mary. Mary observed that her boss spent a lot of his time mentoring her peers in the organization, all who were men. The VP often rode together to a meeting with another director but had never invited Mary to ride with him. Mary decided to ask her boss why he never invited her to ride with him and why he never spent any time mentoring her. She was shocked when the VP said he never rode alone in a car with a female employee because he was paranoid about being accused of sexual harassment.

Even today, this sort of treatment is all too common. This behavior is just one of many subtle actions taken in the workplace which have an impact on limiting a woman's career advancement. I told Mary her boss had probably confided this to her in private, so he could deny it later, if necessary. I also told Mary to consider what additional ways her boss was not supporting her or was not "in her corner."

Mary tried to explain to the VP how unfair it was to her career development to be treated a specific way just because she was a woman. This was clearly an example of gender bias. Mary asked the VP to reconsider his decision, to try and understand the consequences of his actions on her career. Since the VP was not willing to change his behavior, Mary had to decide if the job still exceeded the 51-percent threshold which I discuss in another chapter.

Enhance Your Confidence

> I believe my dad is the original source of my confidence. He taught me how to believe in myself because he believed in me. He pushed me, expected excellence, and delighted in my success. When I stumbled, he said "get up, dust yourself off and keep going!"

Cloene

My children always say, "I have a question, Mom has a book or several books and will read to us or with us and then we have a discussion."

There is a great book recently published titled *The Confidence Code: The Science and Art of Self-Assurance — What Women Should Know* by Katty Kay and Claire Shipman.[2] I really love finding credible material that validates what I already believe! According to Kay and Shipman, "There is a quality that sets people apart. It is hard to define but easy to recognize. With it, you can take on the world; without it, you live stuck at the starting block of your potential … it is confidence that sways people."

The research and science documented in this book answers the question: Which is more important to success — confidence or competence? Confidence is the big winner. The good news from this book is confidence can be learned. Rebecca Elliott, a researcher at the University of Manchester, says, "Fairly simple brain training

---

[2] Kay, Katty, and Claire Shipman. *The Confidence Code: The Science and Art of Self-Assurance — What Women Should Know.* New York: HarperCollins Publishers, 2014.

can carve new pathways in our adult brains, pathways that encourage resilience, or confident thinking, and become part of our hard-wiring." This is because of the new understanding of brain plasticity. Based on her research at the University of Michigan, Professor Nansook Park says: "Brain plasticity is the cornerstone of the idea that confidence is a choice we can all make."

It's very exciting to know that confidence is not just something you are born with or without—luck of the draw. We can learn how to be confident, optimistic, resilient and believe in ourselves *The Confidence Code* is recommended reading for all women and men, whether you are participating in the commercial work place or working at home—particularly if you are raising a daughter. These authors have just published another book *The Confidence Code for Girls*. It is a #1 *New York Times* bestseller and it highly recommended for tween girls.

***

I found I could use support groups to help build and reinforce my confidence. While I was working at Blue Cross in KC, some of my friends and I started a group we called *Women to Women*. I would characterize it as an early women's networking group, among the first in Kansas City. We met at a different member's home each month. At the group's peak, we had 40-plus members, with approximately 20 members attending each monthly meeting.

One of our guest speakers was Kay Barnes, a future mayor of Kansas City. At the time, Ms. Barnes was a member of the City Council in Kansas City. She was also a member of another women's organization called the Central Exchange. This group consisted of many prominent Kansas City women including Adele Hall and Marjorie Powell Allen. At one point, the Central Exchange wanted our group to join them. We declined their invitation and kept our little group going for 5-plus years.

We wanted *Women to Women* to be a place where we could feel comfortable talking to others about what was going on in our lives and careers. It was a support group for women by women. When someone described an issue they faced at work, we all discussed possible ways to address the situation. In addition to career support, we also started a spinoff investment group. We wanted to learn about investing and finance. I don't recall paying any dues for *Women to Women,* but we did have set contributions for the investment club. I do remember refreshments consisted of a punch and some appetizers or treats. The punch was one part Mogen David wine and three parts ginger ale. It was very simple and very cheap. As someone who has developed a preference for good red wine, the recipe for this punch brings back interesting memories. I learned a lot in this group and developed relationships with many of these women which have lasted a lifetime.

If confidence can be taught, then it stands to reason parents can do a lot to enhance the confidence of their children. My father always told me I could do anything I wanted to do with my life; I could be anything I wanted to be if I got an education. This from a man with an 8th grade education. I was an adult before I knew my father had only attended school through the 8th grade. He was well-informed, articulate and confident. I always understood I would go to college—the key to my future success.

My Dad insisted I learn to make my own decisions and accept responsibility for the consequences. I would come home and ask my father if I could do something. My father would say to me: "Well, what do you think?" Frustrated, I would ask him, "Why won't you tell me if it's okay?" His answer was simply, "Well, if you make a bad decision now, I can help you fix it and I know you will learn from the experience. If you make a bad decision when you're 30 years old, I probably won't be able to help fix it. I want you to learn how to make decisions. I want you to learn how to be accountable." As an adult, I remember getting reviews at work with high marks for making quick, decisive decisions. I had lots of practice and I had learned to trust my judgment.

Let your kids try new things, with or without your help, and if they fail, help them get up and try again. The environment in which a young person is raised can enhance or degrade their confidence.

As a parent, if you see your child's confidence wavering, you need to make plans and take steps to enhance their confidence. It will be critical to their success in both their professional and private lives. Read *The Confidence Code* and *The Confidence Code for Girls*.

There are a number of support groups available to young people that can help build confidence. One of my favorites is band. I played clarinet in the marching band at my high school in Booneville. I never intended to continue playing when I went to Ouachita Baptist University. But when I arrived at college, I saw these signs on campus touting the university's marching band. There was a new band director who wanted to field a 100-member marching band. This would be a record for my small school. So I decided to make an appointment to see the band director. I told him about my marching band experience. I was first or second chair clarinet in high school and was really good at marching band. "I am not a music major," I said to him, "I don't have the time or the desire to participate in tryouts. I am willing to sit last chair and will never embarrass you. I just want to be in the marching band." The band director agreed. I had found a community. I was in the marching band. Just like in high school, being in band was a place to instantly belong; a support group. I have recommended this approach to young people. It has many of the same advantages as being on a sport team and helped me build confidence

***

As a child I was overweight. I was 17 when I finally lost 40 lbs. This did not make me slim, but it made me average. I also got contacts and replaced the glasses I had worn since the 3rd grade. I was a singer, a dancer, in plays, and loved performing. I was always conscious of my appearance. I never really had the money to be fashionable.

When I graduated from college and got my first job, I decided I would create my own look. I dressed for the job I wanted and not the job I had. I chose bright colors instead of grey and navy and gradually created a wardrobe of clothes, shoes and jewelry that were my statement. I selected things I liked and really dressed for me. I wore my hair in a style that pleased me and was not time-consuming—not what a guy might like. I kept evolving my look. I was particular about my makeup, my nails. I did things that gave me confidence in the way I looked. I really didn't care what other people thought about my appearance. I only cared about what I thought. I have had a tummy tuck, a face lift, and I have had BO-TOX® injections. I try to keep my weight under control because there is a history of cardiovascular disease in my family. These are things I do for my mental health. I don't apologize for these decisions.

Studies show being well groomed is an asset for both women and men. I have worked with many people who were overweight—even obese—who deal with this disadvantage by being well groomed. They have developed their own look and wear it with style.

I know there is a lot of discussion about how unfair it is that women are judged by their looks. It turns out men are also judged by their looks, even though they are not expected to wear makeup. I believe this is a personal decision. I know women who have decided not to wear makeup or be concerned about how they dress. I respect their right to make that decision. It would not work for me. I like and need the confidence boost I get from being well groomed. For me, it is worth the time and the money.

Confidence Blacklist

- Over-thinking: Learn to make a decision based on the best information you have. If it turns out to be a mistake, make a course correction and keep on going. Own your successes and own your mistakes. This will increase your confidence and credibility.

- People Pleasing: Please yourself and your family first; be true to yourself.

- Inability to let go of defeats: I give myself a time limit on feeling sorry for myself after a defeat. I have taught myself to learn and move on.

- Perfectionism: Perfection is the enemy of good enough.

- Hurt feelings: I don't deny when my feelings are hurt, but I do limit the amount of time to wallow in self-pity before I move on.

- Opting out: Opting out is not an option. You have to find a way to move forward.

- Indecision: If you are struggling with a difficult decision, reach out to a trusted advisor and discuss the options. Own your ultimate decision and the plan to make it work.

- Pessimism: Winston Churchill said, "A pessimist sees the difficulty of every opportunity; an optimist sees the opportunity in every difficulty." It is very difficult to have the energy and attitude to succeed if your glass is always half empty! Be bold. **Be very bold!**

My 51 Percent Rule

> When I am at work, I am all in. I also spend a lot of time at work. So I have one primary guiding principle. I must be deliriously satisfied with my job at least 51 percent of the time or I move on.

Cloene

If I have one primary guiding principle, it's I have to be deliriously satisfied with my job at least 51 percent of the time. Notice I said "deliriously" satisfied. I spend a lot of time at my job and I am not going to be unhappy while I am there. When I am at work, I am all in 100 percent. I do not want to be distracted by factors detracting from my job satisfaction. Most of the jobs I have left have gone from deliriously satisfying to miserable in just a few days.

There are lots of factors which contribute to or take away from your job satisfaction. Many of these will be familiar to you, such as great management, challenging job assignments, compensation, benefits, and respect from your boss and co-workers. You also have to consider time away from your family and flexibility of your work hours.

When I add up all the pluses and minuses, the pluses must be overwhelmingly greater than 51 percent. I have always believed, if I needed to, I could find another job. I also know I cannot be successful unless I like most aspects of my job. When my job satisfaction falls below 51 percent, I start to look for other opportunities.

During my first stint at Trans World Airlines (TWA), I was recruited by a Vice President of information technology at Panhandle Eastern Pipe Line Company. Previously, I had worked with him when he was an application development director at TWA. He wanted me to implement a development methodology at Panhandle Eastern. It was a promotion, plus I really liked this VP and wanted to be part of his organization. However, the job did not report to my mentor. I actually reported to his VP of information technology planning who was definitely not a feminist or even interested in fair play.

On my first day, I discovered he had assigned me to an inner office with a huge support column in the middle. All of my peers, and even some other managers junior to me, had outer offices with windows. There were three empty outer offices with windows. After I had been there for a few days, I went to have a chat with my boss to tell him the office situation wasn't working for me. He proceeded to tell me the three vacant offices were reserved for open positions senior to mine. I decided to hold my ground. I informed him I was going to move into one of those vacant offices. I said, "When you hire someone that you and I both agree is senior to me, and the other two offices are filled, I will move out of the office."

Needless to say, I didn't stay at Panhandle Eastern for very long. I decided it was not a good enough opportunity to put up with the blatant gender bias. I was lucky because a TWA director called and asked me to consider returning to the airline. In a few short months, I was back at TWA.

***

My second time at TWA resulted in one of the most exciting opportunities of my career. TWA management reorganized the information technology (IT) department and James Newkirk became the vice president of IT. I was promoted to director and was the first female director in TWA's IT organization.

After the reorganization, TWA decided to fund a major project to upgrade the 10-year-old frequent flyer bonus system (FFB). We elected to use the Texas Instruments Information Engineering Facility (IEF) software, as well as IBM's DB2, a new database management system. We were in a race with several other corporations to see who could go live first with a system using the IEF software. I was asked to serve on the IEF User Group Board and then received approval from TWA to serve a two-year term as the chairperson of the IEF User Group. There were around 2,000 attendees at the annual conference. I would rate this job at 98.9%. High risk, high reward!

Then TWA had another reorganization and a layoff. I was in Dallas at the annual IEF User conference when I received a call from my new boss who I had never met. He told me to leave the conference and come back to Kansas City to participate in the layoff discussions. I explained that TWA had committed to letting me serve a two-year term as chairperson and I needed to finish the conference. I had already made sure my employees who were losing their positions had been picked up by other parts of the organization and the person I left in charge could represent me in the meetings. I didn't go back.

When I met with him on Monday after returning, he was furious and the meeting was downhill all the way. After about five minutes, I told him I was going to resign. He looked at me and said, "You can't resign!" I replied I was sure I was still in the United States of America and I could resign. In one week I went from 98.9% to 0%.

However, to be honest, I would not have just walked out if I had not had another job offer. I had a responsibility to my family. I would have immediately started a job search and I would have put up with the situation until I found a new opportunity. I was very lucky I already had an offer.

***

When I decided to leave TWA, my experience with information engineering and Texas Instruments' IEF tool brought me a job offer from the consulting firm Computer Task Group (CTG). Before accepting the job, I made certain my boss, Paul Hessinger, agreed to certain conditions. I needed to be home 50 percent of the time. I knew travelling was going to be part of the job but I was not willing to be away from my family more than 50% of the time. He agreed, and we made it work. I spent a lot of my time speaking at conferences. I also visited a lot of client sites to discuss how to succeed using information engineering and tools like IEF.

After a year, I realized being home only half the time was just not good enough. The job was a great opportunity and I learned a lot, but it still did not meet my 51 percent threshold.

***

As I was leaving CTG, I was seriously considering a job with Budget® Rent-a-Car in Chicago. Budget® had offered me a Vice President position in their IT organization to help them implement the IEF software. It would mean moving my family to Chicago. My husband, Tom, had worked and lived in Chicago before and was willing to make the move. My son, Justin, was a teenager about to start high school in Kansas City and not as eager. He was devastated at the thought of moving to Chicago and leaving his friends and school. This was a great opportunity for my career. One of my career goals was to continue moving up the corporate ladder. Vice president was next on the list.

A week before I had to let Budget® know if I was going to accept their job offer, I received a call from a local recruiter I knew very well. Sprint had just hired their first ever chief information officer (CIO). It was Ron Ponder from Federal Express and he was going to report to Sprint's CEO. Ponder was a great fan of data management and was looking for someone to head up his data management organization at Sprint. This recruiter had told Ponder about me and given him my resume. I received the recruiter's call on Friday, met with Ponder on Monday, met with several members of his team on Tuesday and received a job offer on Friday.

The job offer was for a senior director position. To this day, I believe if I had been a man with my credentials, experience and accomplishments, I would have been offered an assistant vice president (AVP) position. I was the only direct report to Ron Ponder who wasn't at least an AVP and the only female direct report.

I knew my family wanted to stay in Kansas City and their happiness was an important part of my 51 percent. So I accepted Sprint's offer.

51 percent is a very personal assessment. I have discussed this idea with other professional friends and several had the idea but a different percent. It is not the percent that is important. It is the idea of continually assessing your job to be sure you are not the "frog in the boiling water" gradually getting hotter and hotter until it dies. Do a regular job satisfaction assessment and proactively decide if you need to start looking for a new opportunity.

***

There are many different components that determine if you're exceeding your 51 percent threshold. One of my important factors is whether I am making a difference. Sometimes a company or organization chooses to discount your input. When this happens to me, it goes into the negative column.

Here is my list of considerations for evaluating my 51 percent. These are not in any particular order of importance. At different times in a career what's in the list and the order of importance will change. For example, when my children were younger, family considerations carried a greater weight than career opportunity.

- Family
- Interesting, exciting work
- Great team of peers
- Great team of direct reports
- Respect for management
- Respect and support from management
- Freedom
- Recognition
- Flexibility
- Total compensation package including benefits

Take Chances, Accept Risk

> When I have to assess a risky decision, I always ask myself, "What is the worst thing that can happen?" Facing this head-on enables me to move on. High risk, high reward!

Cloene

Even the most talented professional cannot demonstrate her value if she only works on low-risk, low-reward projects. I am sure you have heard the old saying, "If it's easy, anyone can do it." One certain way to get noticed and show you are valuable is to successfully complete important projects. There is another benefit of working on critical projects. These are the best projects for learning new skills or honing existing skills. Also, they are a lot more fun!

I am sure some of you are thinking, "But what happens if I fail?" Well, I have never been afraid to fail. You can learn a lot from failure. First you figure out the root causes of the failure. Then you can make the necessary changes to mitigate or remove those causes. This will help you when you take on that next critical project.

My whole career has been one of taking chances and accepting the risks associated with difficult projects. A high-risk project is a lot more exciting; the people you work with are more interesting and challenging; the potential rewards are greater. The best times I have ever experienced at work came from building and managing high-performance teams.

***

Taking a chance is what led me to a career in Information Technology (IT). It happened while I was working for the State of Arkansas.

The state had just signed a contract with IBM to develop an Information System Strategy Plan for Arkansas state government. IBM assigned several senior people to lead the effort. The governor established the Information Systems Executive Committee (ISEC) and assigned members of his cabinet to serve on this committee. ISEC wanted someone who knew state government and asked me to be the program coordinator. I had just finished my tenure as a senior budget analyst in the governor's finance department and had accepted a job on the governor's staff. When I said I didn't know anything about information technology, they told me that was perfect because I wouldn't have any preconceived ideas. They believed in me.

I decided to take a chance. They put me in a room with an IBM Systems Engineer for six weeks, 10 to 12 hours a day, and this person taught me about the science of information technology. We produced the first information system strategy plan for a state government developed in partnership with IBM. The final plan was approved by the governor, his cabinet and the legislature. Examples from this plan were published in a book by James Martin. At that time, Martin was one of the most famous Information Technology gurus of his time and a leading proponent of data resource management. My career in Information Technology centered on these new ideas for managing data as a resource. "Big Data" is the latest hot concept for managing data.

This was when I really started my speaking career. IBM was eager to promote their methodology for developing an Information System Strategy Plan for state governments and wanted to engage with other potential customers. The governor and his cabinet were enjoying all of the positive publicity for the state. IBM sponsored me as a customer speaker at numerous industry conferences where

I explained how we used the IBM methodology to create the Arkansas Information Systems Strategy Plan.

***

The next big opportunity of my career came about because of the skills I learned developing the Information Strategy Plan for the State of Arkansas. In 1978, I accepted a position with the Information Systems organization at Trans World Airlines (TWA). I was going to be responsible for rolling out a software development methodology to their information systems developers. TWA had selected Information Engineering from Knowledgeware as its methodology.

Once again I chose an opportunity to take on something new. At the State of Arkansas, I was the program coordinator during the development of an Information Strategy Plan, which included data management techniques. So there was some overlap, but this job involved implementing a methodology for COBOL program developers.

I learned the details about the Information Engineering (IE) methodology by attending Knowledgeware training sessions and reading a lot of their documentation. We successfully rolled out the methodology at TWA. As a result of our success, Knowledgeware invited me to join their speaker's circuit and talk about implementing information engineering at TWA.

***

TWA's VP for information systems had hired James Newkirk to be AVP of application development. James was building a new team and asked me to be the Director of a new data resource management organization. James was a big proponent of the information engineering methodology. He wanted me to lead the organization that was going to implement information engineering at TWA. My team was responsible for the application development methodology, data analysis, database administration and the information strategy plan. Our first assignment was to deploy a new information systems development platform called the Information

Engineering Facility (IEF) from Texas Instruments. Then we decided to use the IEF methodology and platform to rewrite TWA's Frequent Flyer Bonus (FFB) system.

It was James Newkirk who wanted to use information engineering techniques to redesign the existing FFB system. The original system had been designed to support 100,000 customers and last for six months. Ten years later, the system needed to be replaced to properly support the now over 8 million TWA frequent flyer members.

This was a high-risk, high-reward project. TWA competed with many other airlines and building customer loyalty with a frequent flyer program was one critical component in an airline's success. Now we were going to rebuild FFB using a brand new application development platform.

The technology was so new that no one had yet used it to deploy a system into production. There was a lot at stake. James asked me to be co-program director along with one of his application development directors, and we assigned the best and brightest to work on the project. I jumped at the chance to help lead this high-performance team and show that Information Engineering could deliver results.

I am not going to say it was easy, but we did use information engineering to redesign the FFB system. When we installed the new FFB system into production, we became Texas Instruments' first customer to deploy an application into production using their technology. We were in a race with several other Texas Instruments' customers and only won the race by a few weeks. The publicity machine at Texas Instruments went into full force, and TWA was featured in several magazine articles and industry newspapers. I became a featured speaker at numerous industry conferences.

Over a three-day holiday weekend, we moved all 8 million subscribers to the new platform. After FFB had been in production for less than a year, TWA sold the program to Lufthansa Airlines for an amount that covered the development cost of the redesign.

Texas Instruments representatives encouraged me to become active in the IEF User Group. Eventually, I served on the user group board, and then served as chairperson for two years. As chairperson, I spent a lot of time organizing the user group meetings, particularly the big annual meeting. Attendance at the annual meeting usually approached 2,000 people. I also attended and spoke at the IEF Annual Conference in Europe.

I couldn't have served on the board without the support of my boss and TWA management. The board met four times a year and Texas Instruments asked me to speak at numerous industry conferences. TWA was a success story for IEF, and I stood out from the crowd because I was a woman. At the time, information technology was dominated by men.

I relished these opportunities to speak in front of large groups, improving my presentation skills. I particularly liked the question and answer sessions. When you have these opportunities, you have to make the most of them. Embrace every chance you get to acquire new skills and improve existing skills.

***

One of the biggest opportunities of my professional career happened when I joined Sprint PCS (Sprint's mobile phone division) as the VP of information resource management. Sprint had made the decision to enter the mobile phone market, and Sprint PCS was the result. I joined in the spring of 1996, during the initial systems build out for the new company. I had worked with the Sprint PCS Chief Operating Officer (COO) while he was an executive in Sprint's Local Telecommunications Division. The COO's vision was to build a comprehensive series of data warehouses. If Sprint PCS used the information stored in data warehouses to manage the business from the start, the business would find these warehouses invaluable and continue to fund them as the company grew.

I was asked to join Sprint PCS because of my data management and data warehouse experience. My team was responsible for building out the data warehouses that would be used to manage the business and to support database management for the numerous applications needed to support the business. We did implement the data warehouses envisioned by the COO. We started small in the beginning for a small amount of money and then scaled the platform as the business grew. The day PCS launched in two cities, the executives could see key store sales information on their new digital phones. The COO's belief that the business would find the data warehouses invaluable turned out to be correct. I distinctly remember the time I requested $33 million to support an equipment build out for the ever-growing data warehouses. Each department head I met with basically said, "Well, I can't live without the data warehouses, but I don't think anybody else is using them as effectively as I am." The budget request was approved. Nobody was willing to lose their data warehouses.

Throughout my career, I have had four outstanding opportunities. The first was getting to be the program coordinator for the implementation of the Information Strategy Plan for the State of Arkansas. The second one was bringing the IEF into TWA and implementing a redesigned FFB system. The third was implementing the data warehouses at Sprint PCS, which built the foundation on which Sprint PCS managed their business operations. The fourth was when I was promoted to manage the Application Development organization at Sprint PCS. I had 15 direct reports and 1,200 professionals in the organization—the largest organization I ever led.

These opportunities were great for my career, but also exciting, fun and interesting. They gave me a great sense of accomplishment, being able to do something impactful for the organization. I learned to build and lead high-performing teams. There is nothing more exciting than working with a high-performing team.

Don't Make Yourself Indispensable

> If you want to move up the corporate career ladder, you must always have your replacement identified and in training. It might FEEL good to think that you are indispensable, but if you are a good leader and a good manager you will have a replacement ready to go. Good corporations are rich in talent and have very good succession plans.

Cloene

There is ample research to show many women are not good at delegating. One reason appears to be that for a woman to be successful, they have to be very good at what they do. They are proud to be recognized as an "expert." Do you ever find yourself thinking, "I'm indispensable; I do my job so well, they will never find anybody to do this as well as I do. AND, I will never teach anyone to do it as well as I do." You probably are as safe as anyone can be, but you are also stuck in that job. You may be safe. **Safe and Stuck!**

Over the years I have observed what I call "indispensable women." These women have learned a complex series of tasks. They can accomplish these tasks quickly, with a very low error rate. Often they are promoted to a position in which they lead a team of people performing the tasks. They become subject matter experts—often referred to as specialists—and are leaned on heavily by their organizations. However, their proficiency is an anchor because the organization would find it painful to lose their expertise. The indispensable woman is too valuable in her current position to be promoted. Avoid the indispensable woman trap by making sure you are preparing one or more of your staff to replace you. It may seem counterintuitive, but you cannot move up the ladder unless you have groomed someone to take your place.

I have also found indispensable women are resistant to change. Subject matter experts can stumble when change disrupts their world. I remember a time at Sprint when we were replacing some of the computer systems with new technology. I knew some women there who chose to retire instead of learning the new system. Instead of embracing the change, they worried the change was going to erode their expertise and harm their careers or they had so much invested they couldn't face the hard work to learn new skills. You can avoid this by making sure you are an expert in the underlying business processes and not just how to use tools for performing step-by-step tasks. You can be a change agent instead of someone whose career is harmed by change.

Indispensable women are sometimes lulled into thinking they are helping their careers because they are invited to participate in senior level meetings. When I worked for Disney, there was a woman on the team who was very good at PowerPoint and Excel. She was invited into senior level meetings to produce documents in these programs. She was a very skilled technical administrative assistant but she was not included because they valued her input and opinions. It reminded me of when I started my career and decided never to admit I could type. If they knew I could type 60 words a minute, I'd get lots of typing assignments.

***

The ability to delegate successfully is one of the most important skills every professional woman needs to learn. Moving up the career ladder usually involves leading larger organizations with ever greater responsibilities. To make progress in your career, you must learn how to delegate. You need to learn how to teach others to do the things at which you excel. You need to ensure your team will be successful without you. Only then will you be able to move up to the next, better opportunity that becomes available. If you make yourself indispensable, you are limiting your upward mobility in the organization. Every time I got offered a new opportunity one of the first questions was: "Who would you recommend as your replacement? Are they ready for the job?"

> Humbling to know, there are at least 10 IBM executives who could take my place tomorrow.

IBM CEO

I remember an anecdote told by an instructor for a class I took while working at TWA. The instructor was married and had two small children. He and his wife agreed it was important to have their young children make their beds in the morning. It did not start out very well. The instructor said as far as he was concerned, they did a crappy job making their beds. Without thinking, he found himself going into their rooms and remaking their beds. Pretty soon, the two kids got worse and worse at making their beds. They had figured out Daddy was going to fix it. No matter what they did, it wasn't going to be good enough. The instructor told us he had to come to the realization his standards did not really apply to the situation. If he really wanted for his kids to learn to make their beds in the morning, how they did it had to be good enough for him. He just had to believe it would improve over time. Eventually, they would make their beds to his standard.

There is a lesson here. When you delegate, the result has to be "good enough," even if it doesn't always meet your standards. Instead of doing the job yourself, you have to coach them to improve over time. It's impossible for you to be able to do everything. You must delegate. If you have a job where you can do everything, then it is not a very big job! Big jobs have big rewards.

***

Avoiding the pitfalls of being indispensable works both ways. As a manager of other women, it is important to be a good mentor rather than a selfish boss. While I was a vice president in information technology at Sprint PCS, a woman worked for me as my executive assistant. She had worked for me at TWA then Sprint, and was one of the best assistants I ever had. It's like the old saying; she knew what I needed before I told her. She felt indispensable to me.

One day she came to ask for my support in applying for an analyst job in another department at Sprint. I resisted the urge to try and talk her out of applying for the position. I knew my day-to-day job would be much harder if she left, but I gave her all the help I could to support her decision. She got the job and, indeed, my job was much harder as I began working with a new assistant.

I actually helped two of my best executive assistants get promotions. I hated it. It was painful to lose them. My life was much more difficult while I went through the hiring and training processes. However, they moved into management level positions with bonus opportunities. I was so proud of them.

As a boss, you cannot hold someone back when they want to move up the career ladder. Even when they feel indispensable, you must help your people get ahead. That's part of being a team and being a great leader. Your team has to know you will be there to support them. I always took it as a compliment when members of my team were pursued for advancement opportunities.

Perseverance

> If you believe you are right, someone telling you "No" really just means, "Not right now."

Cloene

I have been accused of being charming when using the power of persuasion to fight for something I believe in. More important, I use a fact-based approach and can be very tenacious when I believe I am right.

I am sure many of you have pitched an idea, only to be told it will never work or, "That's not how we do things here." Or you have been told to take some action, believing it is the wrong approach.

I believe when someone tells you "no," what they are really saying is "not now" or that my proposal was not strong enough. One of my bosses chuckled when he told me, "No never means no to you, does it?" I replied: "Not if I believe I'm right. You pay me a lot of money and I should be able to persuade you if I am right." I had a reputation for being persistent and persuasive.

I have often been able to change no to yes by backing off when I am first told "no." I'll reconsider, do more research to support my argument, and try again. However, it is important to pick your battles. Not everything is worth fighting for.

***

I started using the art of persuasion and persistence very young. Even back then when something was very important to me, I was unwilling to take no for an answer. In an earlier chapter, I described my 8th grade dilemma. I wanted to take World History, but it was offered at the same time as a required class, Home Economics, and I didn't want to take Home Economics.

When I told my mother I did not want to take Home Economics, she laughed at me. My mother expected me to take Home Economics because she expected me to know how to cook, how to sew and do all those things that were "important" for girls to know. The first reaction from my dad was one of resignation. He told me, "I don't know what we can do about this. It's a required subject for graduating from your junior high school." But I didn't take no for an answer.

Instead, I wrote down on paper the options available to fit the history class into my schedule. The only way I could take the history class was if I didn't take home economics. This was my humble attempt at a spreadsheet. I took this paper and showed it to Daddy. Again he said, "All the girls take home economics," but he did listen and looked carefully at my plan. Daddy arranged a meeting with the school's superintendent. I was going to have to convince the superintendent to let me substitute world history for home economics.

Now I am sure the superintendent thought this was a ridiculous notion, but I must say he listened to my explanation. Then he turned to my father and said, "World history is a junior/senior-level class. All the other student will be juniors and seniors. If Cloene takes the class, she will most certainly fail." Daddy's reply was, "She might, but that's okay. Failing can be a powerful lesson. If she succeeds, that will also be a powerful lesson." Because of my persuasion and perseverance and my father's support, I was an eighth grader who took a senior-level world history class instead of home economics. And I didn't fail the history class. I made an A. Now came the hard part, Dad had to tell my Mom I wasn't going to take home economics.

Perseverance and persuasion can also pay off when your plans are not actively opposed, but not given any support. When I was a junior in high school, three of us—two boys and me—were discussing why no one from our school ever had the opportunity to participate in a summer educational program. When we asked our school counselor, she told us no one had ever done this before. Our counselor said she did not know where to start. So we went to the library and started digging, trying to find any information we could about summer programs. We found some programs of interest, filled out the applications, and mailed them in. Since I had no money, I was going to have to rely on a full scholarship. All three of us went to summer programs between our junior and senior years. Only persistence allowed us to achieve our plans. We could have resigned ourselves to the fact students at Booneville High School did not participate in these programs, but we chose not to accept that and were richer for it.

> Charm is a way of getting the answer yes without asking a clear question.

Albert Camus

Then there are times when a frontal assault is the wrong approach and you need to flank the opposition's position. This happened to me when I accepted the position of senior director for information resource management at Sprint. I was hired by the new CIO, Ron Ponder, and he told me to build a world class organization, more like the one he had at Federal Express. My first decision was setting minimum criteria for the people who would be part of my organization. We needed to hire high-quality people because the job required the best and the brightest. Ponder bought into my proposal, but then I met with human resources. The person I met with from human resources told me, "We can't do it. Sprint can't hire the best. The CEO has told us we can't afford the best. We have to settle for average employees." I was dumbfounded and incredulous because I said to her, "Well, we sure got that with you." Not the most politically correct comment I ever made!

I did not take "no" for the answer. We had built a great data management organization at TWA. I knew we could do it at Sprint. So I went back to Ponder and convinced him to let me hire an outside recruiter to help build a world class data management organization.

***

Ron Ponder left to take a position as CIO for AT&T. Ponder's leaving led to a reorganization where I was still in charge of Data Management and reported directly to George Fucui, president of Sprint's Network organization.

I was still the only woman and the only senior director in the room. I remember distinctly two occasions when events conspired to impact my working relationships with some of my peers, making my job all the more interesting and challenging.

One time was when Sprint decided to adopt the vitality curve or forced ranking approach to employee evaluation popularized by Jack Welch, the CEO of General Electric. According to Welch, to keep the organization high performing, you needed to get rid of the bottom 10 percent performers every year. Relative to my peers, my organization was comparatively small, 200 people in an organization totaling 5,000 employees. This policy was put in place just after I had rebuilt the organization and hired a bunch of new people. I didn't believe any of my team were poor performers. We had just gone to a lot of trouble to establish requirements and hired accordingly.

So I went in to talk with my boss and said, "I can't do this. You just let me turn this department upside down and get excellent people. We just went through that process. I don't have 10 percent dead weight. We already pruned them from the organization during the reorg. You don't want a Data Management organization that has 20 people who aren't carrying their load. These people represent the special forces of your organization. At a minimum, they have to be good." Well, I convinced my boss and didn't have to cut anyone from the organization. I left the meeting pleased with the decision.

A short time later at one of his staff meetings, many in the room were complaining about being forced to cut 10 percent from their organizations. Maybe he was annoyed with the whining, but my boss said, "Oh, by the way, Cloene came to me and made a convincing argument that she had just completed rebuilding the Data Management organization, so she doesn't have to meet the bell curve. She can rate her people anywhere she thinks is appropriate." Every single man in that room was angry, and their anger was directed toward me. After the meeting, I asked my boss, "Was that fun?" He replied, "I enjoyed every minute of it." He was well aware he had just made it more difficult for me to work with my peers.

The other occasion occurred during the first time Sprint used a 360 review process. In this process, everyone was reviewed anonymously by their boss, their peers and their subordinates. When the results of my subordinate reviews came back, my boss tells the room at the next staff meeting, "I have the results of the 360 reviews here. It's obvious all of you need to take lessons from Cloene. Hers is excellent and the rest of you have a lot of work to do." Once again, he made it more difficult to work with my peers. I have to be honest. I enjoyed it just a little bit. However, I also learned just how deep the resentment toward "the girl" ran in some of my peers.

My daughter Tara had her own experience with perseverance and persuasion. As she started 9th grade, she met the new music director. Soon it was time to begin practicing for the holiday music program for the upper school. Tara immediately noticed that all of the music the new director was preparing for the program was Christmas music. She decided to talk to him to explain that Barstow had a very diverse student body and the holiday program had always included Hanukkah and Kwanzaa music. Since Tara is Jewish, this was very important to her. The director basically said that he wasn't familiar with music for Hanukkah and Kwanzaa holidays and would not be including this music in the program.

Tara and another student told the music director they would not participate in the holiday program. He was not supportive of their decision. This brought attention to the problem but it was too late to change the program that year. The administration told the music director that the program for the next year must include music recognizing the diversity of the school. The girls persevered and helped to right a wrong. High risk, high reward.

***

How do you make persuasion and persistence pay off? I worked hard to have a good, trusting relationship with my bosses. They came to understand I was motivated for the organization to be the best we could be. I did my homework, put together fact-based arguments and provided examples of success. I used that relationship to promote ideas I believed were important to our success. Also, I was willing to accept the risk of being an innovator. It is a high-risk, high-reward play.

Where Did All the Administrative Assistants Go?

> I never admitted that I could type!

Cloene

Except for one year, from the time I started working as a budget analyst for the State of Arkansas until I resigned as a Disney Vice President (30+ years), I had access to a support team of administrative assistants or had my own executive assistant. Until we started doing email from our desktops, I never admitted that I could type. After all, no one ever asked the "boys" if they could type. As a consultant for CTG in 1990, I did learn PowerPoint so I could develop my own presentations. I never needed to learn Excel at my jobs because the corporate budget department or my executive assistants produced the required Excel spreadsheets. I really could not envision needing to be proficient in Excel. **That was a profound mistake!**

In the seven years of my IT consulting work, one of my biggest problems was not being proficient in both PowerPoint and Excel. I hadn't stayed current with this technology and it came back to bite me. I got lucky again. The owner of the consulting company I contracted with provided entry level people who could help me, but it limited my flexibility and usefulness. I tried to learn Excel, however, to use it in consulting requires a high level of expertise and there is no tolerance for an amateur.

Technology is a given. A level of technical expertise is more and more important to your success and you have to stay on top of it. **If you don't, you will reach a point where it will stall your career. Think of the changes you will be expected to embrace during a**

career most likely spanning 40-plus years AND the next 40 years will see more technological evolution than the last 40 years.

There have been numerous studies showing individuals are resistant to change. Women pursuing professional careers are no exception. There are many reasons why you may resist change. New technologies are disruptive. You have worked hard to be successful with your existing set of tools and technologies. Every time you have to learn a new technology or replace an outdated system with a new version, there is a learning curve and it will take time to redevelop your expertise. It's very important to embrace the changes resulting from new technologies. If you're resistant to change, you have become part of the problem instead of part of the solution.

PART 4—FINANCIAL PLANNING

I included this section on Financial Planning because I don't want any of you to make the mistakes I made. I hate confessing how really uninformed I was and it cost me dearly. I didn't manage my wealth like I managed my family and career.

When I Screw Up, I REALLY Screw Up

What Cloene Could Have Done

When I Screw Up, I REALLY Screw Up

> Outsource your financial decisions and get help from an experienced financial advisor.

Cloene

One of the most important reasons for writing this book is to share with you the mistakes I made in managing my money. I hope this section will help you avoid my tragic (maybe sad is a better word) and mostly avoidable mistakes. I have asked my financial advisor and CERTIFIED FINANCIAL PLANNER™ (CFP®), Brook Deaver, to contribute to this section. I have finally outsourced financial management to an expert. Funny it took me so long to figure this out.

My parents worked for the State of Arkansas all of their adult lives. Part of their compensation was a state pension when they retired. And of course, they had Social Security. I don't believe my parents ever owned a share of stock.

My first jobs after college consisted of a stint as a VISTA volunteer, as an instructor for the Opportunities Industrialization Center (OIC) and several positions for the State of Arkansas in Little Rock. No bonuses or stock options were part of any of these compensation packages. I assumed I would work somewhere and retire with a pension.

My biggest financial mistakes happened while I worked for Sprint and after my divorce. My husband was a CPA and had a successful career at IBM. So, while we were married, he was my financial advisor. While I was a Director at TWA, I was eligible for the stock options program but the company never made enough of a profit to pay out any bonuses or options while I was there. However, when I worked at Sprint, I did receive grants of options and once of stock. As it turns out, I didn't understand all of the details and made some poor decisions.

By 1992, when I started at Sprint and rolled over my TWA 401(k), I had acquired a few "truths" about investments:

- Make "blue chip" investments and don't sell unless you really need the money. Let it grow. Actually, with our IBM investment, that turned out not to be a bad assumption, but it is not a universal truth.

- Don't sell a stock until your taxes will be treated as long term capital gains instead of ordinary income.

During my time at TWA and the early years at Sprint, there were a lot of changes in how employees saved for retirement. I enrolled in TWA's 401(k) plan when it was offered. It had an employer matching component and the choices for investment were one or two mutual funds. Managing my Sprint 401(k) got more and more complicated as additional investment options were added and everyone talked about the need to diversify and not have all of your savings in company stock. It got really complicated for me when, in 1996, I became a Vice President at Sprint PCS.

As a vice president for Sprint PCS my bonus potential was significantly greater than as a senior director. At Sprint, I received cash bonuses and stock options. I never got stock as a bonus. One year at PCS, I received a large bonus in the form of Sprint PCS stock. The day the stock was issued it was valued at over $600,000. I assumed I should treat this like I did my stock options. I could hold on to the stock for a year so any gains would be taxed as long term capital gains. I did not realize that stock received as a bonus is treated differently by the IRS. When you receive stock as a bonus, it's just like receiving a cash bonus. The value of the stock on the day it is granted is taxed as if it were ordinary income. So I planned on holding on to the stock for at least a year. Sprint PCS stock value was flying high at close to $80 a share, and everything looked great.

Then a number of events occurred, driving down the price of the stock. The merger between Sprint and WorldCom fell through. When it was time to pay income taxes the next year the PCS stock was no longer worth enough to pay the taxes on the bonus. I ended up having to exercise Sprint options to pay my tax bill. Had I understood that the stock was taxable based on the value the day it was issued, I could have paid off my house and other debts. Because I was ignorant of the tax consequences of my bonus, it cost me a lot of money.

Another form of compensation I received was in the form of stock options. These stock options granted me the right to buy the Sprint PCS stock at a set price, no matter what the current stock price was. I went to talk to a friend of a friend who happened to be a financial advisor. He convinced me to borrow money so I could exercise the stock options. I was going to hold on to the stock for a year or more in order to realize long term capital gains. I was convinced the stock price was going to keep going up.

As you may have guessed, this was the same time as the previously mentioned market downturn. When the stock price fell below a certain point, the lender called in the loan. I was convinced my company's stock price was going to rebound. So instead of selling the stock, I decided to pay off the loan with other money. The market downturn continued and the stock price tanked. If I had sold the stock when the lender called the loan, there would have been more proceeds from the sale with which to pay off the loan. **Big mistake.**

Being part of the launch of Sprint PCS was one of the most rewarding career experiences I ever had. So I fell in love with the stock and became emotional instead of rational. This stock went from $78+ a share to less than $5.

I wasn't smart about my finances. It wasn't something I was interested in learning about or spending time on. Some of the people who worked for me had very elaborate spreadsheets they checked every day and some made good decisions because they stayed on top of the stock price fluctuations. I was a single mom taking care of two kids and had a very demanding job working 50 to 60+ hours a week. I also want to say that there were men who made many of the same mistakes I did. I won't mention names but I will say "dumb" in managing money can be gender neutral.

It's important for you to make smart decisions about money because it's very difficult to anticipate all of the events that might happen in the future. And sometimes things happen which make it very difficult to recover from poor decisions. Brook is going to take my experience and offer his perspective for how to make better decisions. So I strongly recommend you outsource your financial decisions and get help from an experienced financial advisor.

What Cloene Could Have Done

By Brook Deaver, CFP®, MBA

> Managing your financial affairs is complicated, particularly what to do with the various forms of compensation you may receive from your employer. I have asked my financial adviser, Brook S. Deaver, CFP®, MBA, from Infinitas to write this chapter describing what steps I could have taken to avoid the financial mess I got myself into.

Cloene

We are going to review several strategies that would have been helpful to Cloene when she was making decisions on how to handle the compensation and incentives she received in the form of company stock and stock options. Understanding all of the tax intricacies and financial planning implications of the various stock accumulation, management, and liquidation methods is a daunting and time-consuming task, requiring the expertise of a tax professional, a human resources professional, and a financial advisor with expertise in this particular area.

One component of long term financial success is to consistently make wise decisions over a long period of time on the day-to-day small, medium, and large financial decisions in your life. A second important component to success is to avoid making really bad decisions on the big financial items that you encounter over time in your life. Ok, so I've just stated the obvious. However, many people neglect to put in the time and energy to develop a competent team to help ensure they indeed make wise decisions and avoid making really bad ones! They don't plan to fail, they fail to plan! A tax professional fills the role of the expert on tax law. A human resources professional can answer questions about the benefit/compensation plans, provide documents that outline the rules of these plans, and connect the tax professional and financial advisor to third-party experts that partner with the employer to create and implement these types of plans. A financial advisor develops and updates a comprehensive roadmap that defines the path and tracks progress toward achieving the client's goals, helps the client make sense of the many moving/competing financial components in their lives, and has experience to know what questions need to be answered in order to make the wise decisions that can greatly improve the client's financial outcomes.

Cloene stated that there were some people that stayed on top of the details of managing their stock and option holdings. They had an adequate combination of time, curiosity, and energy required to navigate the complicated decisions associated with these benefit plans. I'm sure some did this on their own and others engaged their team (tax and human resource professionals, and financial advisor) to assist them. As Cloene stated, she certainly didn't have the time, curiosity, and energy to do this on her own. She should have engaged a competent team of professionals to help her!

One additional and critical point is as follows: the team of professionals can only care as much about a client's financial life/goals/plan as the client does. The client has to meet the team "half-way" by making their financial life and decisions a priority. Over the years I've seen and experienced relationships and outcomes that are restrained by a client who isn't engaged enough in their own financial plan and future.

Every individual's financial situation is different. I cannot provide generic advice that fits every situation. That's why I recommend you enlist the services of a financial professional. But I can discuss what advice I would have given Cloene in her situation. Let's begin by discussing the bonus she received in PCS Stock.

To set the stage, think back to the mid/late 1990s to what was happening in the U.S. stock market. Stocks were having a historic run! The internet revolution that had started in the late 1980s or very early 1990s was well under way. Worker productivity was advancing dramatically due to the technology revolution. The software that could now be built had put the power/ability to trade stocks into the hands of anyone with access to a computer and an internet connection. This was indeed an exciting time!

Sprint PCS in particular was growing rapidly due to both the fact that it was a young, start-up venture and because wireless phone technology had advanced significantly. Therefore, PCS stock was also rapidly advancing, stringing together multiple years of positive stock performance. As Cloene stated in the previous chapter, her work at Sprint PCS was very rewarding. She fell in love with the stock. She became emotional about it and overly optimistic. Not having enough knowledge about these complicated tax rules and being overly optimistic prevented her from making a rational, prudent plan for this significant financial asset.

Cloene received a significant amount of additional compensation in the form of a stock bonus. She should have invested the time to create and engage a competent team to help her develop and recommend a strategy for these shares of stock. As her financial advisor I would work with the tax and human resource professionals to help ensure the right questions are asked and answered. The first and most critical item would be to understand the tax implications and rules associated with receiving the stock bonus.

Upon determining that the stock bonus would be taxed as current year ordinary income, I would have worked with Cloene and her tax professional to determine the amount of taxes that would soon be due on this compensation. She could have sold enough stock immediately to cover the amount of taxes owed. The period of time until the taxes need to be paid is very short. Less than a year is a very short time horizon for financial assets. There is no reason to take any investment risk on this portion of the assets. In my opinion the risk of not having the money to pay the taxes owed far out-weighs the benefit of any additional investment return that might be obtained from these dollars. Let's assume that Cloene's marginal tax rate was 33% for state and federal taxes. She could have imme-diately sold $200,000 worth and put it in the bank for the upcoming tax payment (or she could have elected to make a tax estimate pay-ment if required). She then still has $400,000 of assets to plan for.

The next step would be to review the appropriate amount of liq-uid, short-term assets that Cloene had on hand. As a general rule one should have three to six months of income in liquid assets that can be available within a few days. The three months is the "science" part—everyone should have this much on hand or have a plan to get this amount in liquid savings. At least one month of living ex-penses should be at the bank. Return "of" your money at the bank is more important than return "on" your money at the bank. The rate of return matters less. Virtually instant accessibility and no principal risk matter more. The three to six months portion of the living expenses is the "art" part. If there is more risk or dependence associated with one's income then they need to have closer to six months, creating a larger cushion/reserve. Cloene was a single mom at the time. She didn't have a back-up income if she got sick or hurt or lost her job. She had a "big" job. It might have taken more time to find another "big" job if she lost her job. For these reasons it probably would make sense for Cloene to have closer to six months of living expenses in a liquid reserve. Another considera-tion would be to evaluate the strength of her short term disability coverage. If she had strong short term disability coverage, maybe she could have a little less of a reserve. If the plan provided only limited protection of her income, then she should have a little more in reserve.

As I stated earlier, one or two months is probably enough to have at the bank if we are in a low interest environment like we have been in for a number of years (as a point of reference, note that this is being written in early 2018). The rest of the liquid, accessible cushion could be invested "beyond the bank" in investments that have the potential for more return over time. The type of investments that are often appropriate for the "beyond the bank" strategy have moderate risk and volatility characteristics. Over time the investment return could be markedly higher, but even with some volatility most of the principal could be expected to be there. Cloene and I would find the right balance of risk and reward on these "beyond the bank" assets and then invest them appropriately.

Let's assume that Cloene's liquid reserve fund required $50,000 of her assets. Therefore, after $200,000 for taxes and $50,000 for her liquid reserve, she still has $350,000 of stock to develop a plan for!

From a planning perspective, now that we have accounted for the near-term tax liability, have appropriately funded a liquid and accessible reserve of assets, and we decided not to use any of the remaining assets to immediately pay down any of Cloene's debt, we can consider the remaining $350,000 of stock to be a long term financial asset. Because this asset is in concentrated stock, rather than a more diversified portfolio of assets, we need to carefully manage the potential volatility associated with such a concentrated holding. So, what do we do?

We could incorporate this new asset into Cloene's retirement income plan and reassess how close or far we are from achieving her retirement goal. After all, most people working today desire to be financially independent someday so they can then choose to work or not work on their own terms. What a wonderful position to be in someday! Let's assume that the plan shows that with her planned ongoing savings, these additional Sprint stock assets, and a reasonable long term rate of return, she is indeed on track to achieve her financial independence goal. Knowing this, the important question is how we should manage this large stock position. I want to introduce the concept of an equity collar and then have us look at three scenarios: the stock goes up, the stock stays flat, and the stock goes down.

The equity collar strategy is created by simultaneously buying a put option and selling (or writing) a call option[1]. Now I just said a lot in that last sentence. Here is a brief explanation of the options utilized.

- Buying a put: buying the right but not the obligation to sell a given stock at a given price by a certain time.

- Selling or writing a call: you take on the obligation of selling a given stock at a given price before the option expires. In other words you sell someone the right to buy the stock you own, at a predetermined price.

A required disclosure about options before we continue: Options are not suitable for all investors. Typically, commissions are charged for options transactions. Transaction costs may be significant in multi-leg option strategies, including collars, as they involve multiple commission charged. Please contact your financial advisor for a copy of the Options Disclosure Document (ODD).

Let's now review the benefit/outcome of this strategy: a) it establishes a minimum price and maximum price at which shares of stock will be sold, and b) it is inexpensive to implement because the cash one receives into their investment account by selling the call option, can offset most if not all of the cost of the put option. Implementing an equity collar strategy is a tool that could be beneficial (provided it is properly executed and monitored) for all three of the following scenarios.

The Stock Goes Up: Let's assume that Sprint PCS as a company continued to perform well and the stock continued to climb higher. We should monitor the valuation metrics of the stock using measures such as Price-Earnings Ratios, Price-Earnings-Growth ratios, comparison to peer growth rates and valuation, etc. to determine if the stock is reasonably priced at these higher levels or if it is becoming "too" expensive. If the stock valuation metrics indeed indicated that it was becoming expensive, Cloene could have begun to sell some of the stock. We could pick a percentage that "feels right" as there is no perfect answer here. Let's say we decided to sell 25% of the position. At this point we would consider the tax impact. However the tax impact would be a secondary consideration to the primary consideration—our decision to sell based on valuation. By selling 25% of the position we have locked in an additional gain. No one ever went broke taking a profit! The proceeds from the stock sale could be invested in other prudent ideas that could also improve Cloene's portfolio diversification. Now that we had determined that the stock was already expensive, we could implement a put option strategy to help protect against the downside risk and continue to hold the remaining 75% of the stock. If the stock still continued higher, we could potentially sell the remaining 75% over time at higher prices. It is important to note that while we may be able to sell the remaining stock at a higher price, if the call option is exercised (per the "collar strategy" described on the previous page), the appreciation of the underlying stock would be capped at the strike price we selected. The shares would be sold and the appreciation above that strike price would no longer apply.

The Stock Stays Flat: Sometimes a particular stock won't move higher or lower for an extended period of time. Our plan in this case could include the following: A) monitor Sprint PCS's prospects and financials to determine whether or not we felt there was a catalyst that could move the stock higher or lower. B) Identify other timely investment opportunities that may give us better performance and more diversification. We would then periodically make hold or sell decisions.

The Stock Goes Down: This scenario is the most important reason to have a current retirement income plan in place. Such a plan gives us a framework that we can use to make investment decisions. Without such a plan we are much more likely to make decisions based on hope and emotion. The plan allows us to make fact-based decisions based on Cloene's retirement goal. We hope that Sprint PCS stock continues to climb higher. But if it doesn't we could have discussed and implemented a plan to begin selling the stock before it created too costly of an impact to her retirement plan and goal. There were certainly ways to mitigate the huge loss that Cloene ultimately experienced. Tax consequences do matter. However they are only part of the factors that we consider when planning and making investment decisions. Taxes are never the only factor to consider.

There is tremendous value in developing a plan that can serve as a framework for making financial decisions. It requires time and effort, but it's worth it! This type of planning likely could have kept Cloene from incurring the huge loss that she experienced. Now let's consider how we could have managed her stock options.

Cloene participated in an **incentive stock option** (ISO) plan at Sprint PCS. As a result, Cloene received a quantity of ISOs giving her the right, but not the obligation, to purchase a share of stock at a specific price within a specific period of time. ISOs are issued on the grant date. The ISOs commonly have an expiration date 10 years after the grant date. There is a vesting schedule which dictates how long the options must be owned prior to being eligible for exercise. The option holder can exercise the ISOs by paying the strike price, which was the fair market value of the underlying stock at the time of the grant.

There are a number of ways to exercise an ISO. You can dip into your bank account and pay cash to exercise, trading in the ISOs for stock. As Cloene was advised to do, you can borrow money to obtain the cash needed to exercise the options. Or you can use what is known as a cashless exercise, i.e., immediately selling enough stock to cover the total exercise cost. You can also perform a swap, using the value of existing ISO stock to exercise additional ISOs. Once an ISO option is exercised, you may hold the stock as long as you wish or you may sell the stock at any time.

What makes ISOs popular is their potential to qualify for favorable tax treatment. Whether or not your ISO stock sale qualifies depends on the length of time between the sale, grant and exercise dates. A **qualified disposition** occurs when the ISO stock is sold at least two years after the grant date **and** the ISO stock is sold at least one year after the ISO was exercised. If the ultimate sale of the ISO stock is a qualified disposition, the gain (or loss) is reported as a long term capital gain (or loss) rather than being taxed as ordinary income at the taxpayer's marginal income tax rate. And note that for most ISO owners' long term capital gains tax rates are currently much lower than the corresponding ordinary income tax rate. This is very good news for ISO owners!

But there's more to the story. Even though the grant of ISOs is a form of incentive compensation, the IRS does not immediately consider it taxable income. When you do exercise the ISOs, the IRS still does not consider the exercise to be a taxable event. One of the few exceptions to that statement is when you do exercise ISOs, the difference between the stock's market value and the ISO exercise price is called the **bargain element** and may trigger (or be included in) the alternative minimum tax (AMT).

Now I hope you are beginning to understand why I recommend getting advice from an expert—It's complicated! With this background, let's discuss how Cloene could have handled her ISOs.

***

Cloene had received a grant of ISOs, and upon exercising the options, she wanted to hold the ISO stock for at least a year so she could obtain long-term capital gains tax treatment, i.e. a qualifying disposition. This is a logical strategy. However, this isn't a comprehensive strategy. It doesn't account for what could go wrong. She certainly hoped that the stock would continue to go up or at least stay near the same price. After all, Sprint and Sprint PCS were having great success. That certainly was one possible outcome. But, what if the stock began to move down in price? How much money could she lose? More importantly, how much could she lose knowing she borrowed money to exercise the ISOs? Yikes, there is a great deal of risk here! Well, as Cloene previously stated, the worst case scenario is exactly what happened—the stock moved down rapidly!

If someone has a meaningful portion of their net worth or investment assets in one stock/company we refer to this as "concentrated". When dealing with concentrated stock and option positions you absolutely have to have a plan for managing the risk. I've seen too many friends, co-workers, and clients paralyzed by the possibilities. They fail to make any decision because they aren't sure of the right decision. The right decision is to have a plan in place so that you indeed make a decision as the future plays out over time. And although a more detailed discussion is outside the scope of this chapter, it is worth stating that one of the most important aspects of managing your financial affairs is to have a comprehensive financial plan that is a guide and a playbook for achieving your financial goals. The plan for managing a concentrated stock/option position should be driven by your broader and comprehensive financial plan. We covered some of the components of a comprehensive plan when we discussed her Sprint PCS stock earlier in this chapter. Having clearly defined financial goals, and knowing how close or far you are to being on track to achieve those goals are critical components of a comprehensive financial plan. The plan for a concentrated position must address both what you think will happen (which is often what you want to have happen- because that is how our brains are wired), and the opposite of what you think will happen. In other words, we have to have a strategy covering all of the possibilities.

Cloene's goal was to exercise the ISOs and then sell the ISO stock after it qualified for favorable tax treatment. This meant once she exercised the ISOs, Cloene needed to hold the ISO stock for one year in order to achieve the qualified disposition. If the stock stayed at about the same price we have a simple, carefree 12-month period! She sells the stock after the end of the 12-month period and her gain is taxed at long-term capital gains rates instead of being taxed as ordinary income. Perfect! But Cloene needs plans to cover two additional scenarios.

Scenario 2: What to do if the stock goes up during the 12-month period?

Let's discuss scenario number two where the stock continues to move up during the 12-month period. At what point should Cloene consider selling her ISO stock? Cloene wants to hold the stock for 12 months to pay less tax via the long-term capital gains rate. If the simple, carefree scenario is perfect, Cloene could have used that as her baseline for scenario number two.

To do this, we calculate the two possible tax outcomes at the time the ISOs are exercised. Calculate the realized capital gain for selling the ISO stock immediately. Then estimate the amount Cloene would pay if the gain were taxed as a long-term capital gain, the most favorable outcome. The difference between the realized gain and the favorable tax liability is Cloene's net proceeds from the simple, carefree scenario, Cloene's original goal.

Armed with this information, Cloene's plan will be to sell all (or at least a good portion) of her ISO stock if the price increases enough during the 12 month period when her net proceeds after tax (even though taxed as ordinary income) would equal the net proceeds from the simple, carefree scenario. Once these basics are calculated and understood, there are many additional variations of this scenario that could be implemented. But again, the idea is to develop a pre-set strategy that makes sense so you are prepared to take action.

Scenario 3: What to do if the stock goes down during the 12-month period?

By far, the plan for scenario number three is the most important for two key reasons. First, Cloene was not expecting the stock price to go down, and our brains often cause us to make poor decisions (including no decision) when the unexpected occurs. Second, she had borrowed money to exercise the ISOs, so a large decrease in the stock price could have a disastrous impact on her financial situation.

At a minimum, her plan should calculate an "I must sell all my stock right now" price! This is the share price where the proceeds from the sale of the stock are enough to pay off her tax liability and the principal and interest on her loan. Yes, this is the worst case scenario. Cloene receives zero dollars from the ISO stock after satisfying these liabilities, but at least she wouldn't have to come up with money from other sources/assets. I am sure Cloene agrees this worst case scenario would have been a better outcome than what actually happened.

Additionally, Cloene's plan could have included a downside price that would have still provided a nice/reasonable gain on the

ISOs. The ISOs were probably part of her compensation on top of her base salary. Even if she isn't able to net a gain on top of the ISO portion of her salary, she should still want to protect against losing too much of it. Like many things in life, this is more art than science. But, we should ask the question ahead of time: what is the maximum amount (of my salary, in this case I am willing to lose? That should be the price at which you sell all of your ISO stock.

***

So again, I would have worked with Cloene to develop a thoughtful plan to address her near term tax liability, but also to address those three possible future scenarios. What am I going to do if the stock moves higher? What am I going to do if the stock stays near the current price? What am I going to do if the price goes down? The answers to these questions could also include a time component which laid out specific future dates upon which a specific action would be taken to buy, sell, or hold, some of the stock based on the current price at that time. Systematically reducing a concentrated stock (or option) position over a period of time/years makes sense on many fronts: it results in improved portfolio diversification and it spreads the tax liability of realized gains across multiple years.

In closing, I want to remind us that whether we like it or not, *money* is a very important component in all of our lives - money does indeed make the world go around. We should embrace this truth and also recognize that this fact is not lost on savvy well-paid marketers. The marketing messages constantly bombarding us include: "you can have it all; you can have it right now; you deserve it; everyone else is getting their share; something is wrong with you if you aren't getting your share". Be aware of these messages and learn how to appropriately process them in the context of and for the benefit of your financial well-being! The truth is that our country is in a retirement savings crisis. Most people are not on track to live the same lifestyle in retirement that they are living (or did live) during their working years. Saving and planning doesn't come naturally to most of us. Train yourself to think of financial planning as a life long journey: a series of financial decisions made over a long period of time. Then challenge yourself to allocate more time to this important component of your life so that you make the right decisions along the way. Finally, consider asking an experienced financial advisor to partner with you on your journey.

I'm thankful that Cloene asked me to participate in this project. I'm hopeful that learning about her experience and reflecting on some of the sound advice provided in this chapter will be beneficial to you!

Required Disclosures:

- The examples in this chapter are hypothetical and are for illustrative purposes only. No specific investments were used in these examples. Actual results will vary. Past performance does not guarantee future results.

- Diversification does not assure a profit or protect against loss in declining markets, and diversification cannot guarantee that any objective or goal will be achieved.

- Investments are subject to risk, including the loss of principal. Because investment return and principal value fluctuate, shares may be worth more or less than their original value. Some investments are not suitable for all investors, and there is no guarantee that any investing goal will be met. Past performance is no guarantee of future results. Talk to your financial advisor before making any investing decisions.

HAVE THE CONFIDENCE TO PURSUE YOUR PASSIONS

> It is critical to have confidence and trust in your decisions as you juggle family and career.

Cloene

In this book I have described my journey from growing up in a small town in northwestern Arkansas to the executive suites at Fortune 100 companies. Along the way I also pursued my passion to have a family and helped raise two wonderful children. I chose to have a family and a career, and did what was necessary to achieve both. It was complicated, but I am living proof that it is possible to juggle priorities and have both a career and a family.

If you are passionate about having a family **and** a career, you have to realize you can't harness the power of your passions unless you clearly embrace them. You have to decide what's really important in your life—establish your priorities, develop a plan and execute your plan every day. This is how you find the time to devote to your family, your career and yourself.

One of the most important steps you can take is to **have confidence in your decisions** (page 30) as you juggle family and career. It's stressful when you think you are spending too much time at work and not enough with your family, or vice versa. It's even worse when the people you look to for support criticize your decisions.

When I first read the following excerpt from Brené Brown's book, it brought tears to my eyes:

Susan was in her late twenties when we met. She had been married for three years and had a daughter who had just celebrated her first birthday. Susan had loved her career as a physical therapist but had spent the previous year at home with her baby. As family finances grew tighter, she had decided to return to work part-time. In our interview she recalled the day when she thought the right job had landed in her lap. She remembered being absolutely ecstatic. Not only had she been offered a perfect part-time physical therapist position, but her church had an open slot for her daughter in their Mother's Day Out program. Anxious to share her good news, she called her older sister. Rather than congratulating Susan, her sister responded to the news by saying, "I'm not sure why you even had a child if you're not interested in raising her." Susan remembers feeling like she had been punched in the stomach. She said, "I could hardly breathe. It was devastating. My first thought was 'I'm a bad mother.' By the evening, I was considering refusing the job offer.[3]

Too often those we turn to for support respond by shaming and judging. My advice when this happens is:

- Let go of what other people think
- Let go of perfect; embrace good enough
- Let go of striving to be super woman, get help
- Let go of mom-shaming

Only you know what is good enough. If you find yourself feeling guilty about something, go back and reaffirm you are making the best available choices. This will help restore your confidence in the face of adverse criticism.

---

[3] Brown, Brené. *I Thought It Was Just Me (but It Isn't): Telling the Truth About Perfectionism, Inadequacy, and Power.* New York: Gotham Books, 2007.

Be **resilient** (page 35) in the face of adversity. Not every decision you make will turn out well; there will be some disappointments. Find opportunity in these setbacks. Resilience is a valuable attribute for you and important to teach to your children.

In managing family and career, how you allocate the finite resource of time is your most challenging decision every day. Only spend your personal time and energy on what's really important for you to do. For the myriad other family tasks that have to be done, rely on family and friends for some then **outsource** (page 38) by hiring others to do the rest. Maybe you can't make every soccer practice or voice lesson, but you will make sure they get to the practices and lessons and that you get to the soccer games and recitals. Prioritize!

As you move up the career ladder and your children start school, there will be additional demands on your time from external groups. You may be asked to become active in your favorite nonprofit organization or one of the extracurricular school groups. You may want to participate in these activities but only you can decide if you have enough time. If these do not align with your passions, you have to **learn how to say no** (page 44) to yourself and then to others.

Many women who are great managers at work resist using those same skills to **manage their family life** (page 47). Even decisions about how big a family to have must be prioritized based on your personal passions. These decisions can greatly impact your time commitments. I consciously decided to have only two children and had those six years apart. I was able to have a great family and still had time to devote to my career. If you want a larger family, more power to you! Just realize family will take a larger portion of your time, often to the detriment of your career.

In my first job interview after graduating from college, I encountered blatant **gender bias** (page 51). I knew right then and there that job was not one I was interested in. Then I interviewed for a job with the State of Arkansas. Again I encountered gender bias but because I was very interested in the job, I decided to address the gender bias head on. I did so in a dispassionate and professional manner. This approach to dealing with gender bias led to increased respect and new opportunities. As I said in an earlier chapter, I am an unapologetic feminist and believe everyone should be a feminist. Fathers, mothers, brothers, sisters, partners, sons, and daughters should all believe in equality. In the workplace, this means equality of pay, opportunity, access and influence.

I began this chapter by recognizing **confidence** (page 61) is key to juggling your family and career. In the book *The Confidence Code* there is scientific proof that confidence can be learned. In your career, you might be surprised to learn that confidence is even more important to success than competence. As your confidence grows, you can learn how to help your children have greater confidence. Also seek out women's organizations in your area where you can meet other women with the same passion for family and career. You can share ideas and lessons learned. There is strength in numbers.

I learned confidence and resilience when I was a child because my parents supported my decisions to take on challenges at school. They knew if I failed the challenge, I would learn some valuable lessons. I would learn how to be resilient and also how to do it better the next time. Check out the appendix for additional reading to help you enhance your own confidence.

When you devote so much of your time and energy to your career, make sure you are in jobs that make you happy. Throughout my career I followed a simple rule of thumb—I have to be deliriously satisfied with my job at least **51 percent** (page 67) of the time. If not, it's time to find a new job. When I am at work, I am all in, 100-plus percent. I do not want to be distracted by factors detracting from my job satisfaction. Understand what about your job makes you satisfied and what detracts from that satisfaction. Whether your number is 51 percent or 75 percent or whatever, it's important to be very satisfied more than half the time.

Being successful means **taking chances** (page 72). At work, challenging, risky projects give you the opportunity to demonstrate your value and learn new things. No matter how talented you are, no one will recognize your talent if you only work on low-risk, low-reward projects. I am sure you have heard the old saying, "If it's easy, anyone can do it." One certain way to get noticed and show you are valuable is to successfully complete important projects. There is another benefit of working on critical projects. These are the best projects for learning new skills or honing existing skills. Also, they are a lot more fun!

The flipside of not taking chances is to be perceived as **indispensable** (page 78). Many women make this mistake and find their boss is unwilling to support their advancement. When you are in a management position, make sure you are grooming someone to replace you. How else will you be able to move up the career ladder, if there's no one to take your current place? One way to groom members of your team is by delegating important tasks. To make progress in your career, you must learn how to delegate. You need to learn how to teach others to do the things at which you excel. When you delegate, the result has to be "good enough," even if it doesn't meet your standards. Instead of doing the job yourself, you have to coach them to improve over time. This is how to ensure your team will be successful without you. Then you can continue your move up the career ladder.

Sometimes when you run into headwinds at work, you will find it necessary to **persevere** (page 82). When I was arguing for an idea I really believed in, I used a fact-based approach and was very tenacious, even when they said no to my idea. To me that "No," really just meant, "Not right now." I reconsidered, did more research to support my argument, charmingly tried again and again, and more often than not got a "Yes." Perseverance is a powerful tool to accomplish things that will enhance your career. But it is important to pick your battles because not everything is worth fighting for.

Throughout my career, the role of **technology** (page 82) in the office has seen dramatic changes and has brought with it many new tools. Sometimes you can find learning how to use these tools overwhelming. In the past, directors and executives could rely on an executive assistant to use these tools on their behalf. That's no longer the case. Developing a level of technical expertise is becoming more and more important to your success. If you don't, you will reach a point where it will stall your career. Don't forget to stay on top of the key technologies in your profession.

Earlier I described how you should outsource to save valuable time for spending on your passions. But outsourcing is also useful when you do not have the expertise to perform certain key life tasks. In the last two chapters of my book, I shared how I learned an expensive lesson—when you don't understand certain aspects of your compensation package, it pays to **outsource your financial decisions to a professional** (pages 91 and 95). As you move up the career ladder, you will likely receive company stock and stock options as part of your compensation package. The tax implications for such grants are complicated and I highly recommend using a financial professional to help you understand this and help you make good decisions.

Throughout my book I have described what decisions I made and what actions I took in order to have a family and a career. I have learned a lot along the way and have tried to impart some of this hard-earned wisdom to you. It's important you understand my passions may or may not be the same as yours. Understanding what my passions were, I was able to put together a plan that allowed me to have a wonderful family and a successful career. I made decisions based on my need to achieve my desire for a successful, meaningful career and a family. I love my children and I immensely enjoy being a mom and now a grandmother. It is an essential part of who I am. Just as being successful in the workplace is an essential part of who I am.

It is hard work to understand your passions, but once you do you can make the decisions to help you reach your goals. I hope this book will help guide you to success.

APPENDIX: BOOKS I HIGHLY RECOMMEND

> Ask a question, Mom has a book—or books—and will read to us or with us and then we have a discussion.

Cloene's Kids

During the process of writing this book I have read numerous books and articles about family and career. These are the titles I highly recommend to help you learn more about juggling family and career.

Family

Alcorn, Katrina. *Maxed Out: American Moms on the Brink*. Berkeley, CA: Seal Press, 2013.

Brown, Brené. *I Thought It Was Just Me (but It Isn't): Telling the Truth About Perfectionism, Inadequacy, and Power*. New York: Gotham Books, 2007.

———. *Men, Women & Worthiness: The Experience of Shame and the Power of Being Enough*. Audiobook. Boulder, CO: Sounds True, 2012.

———. *The Gifts of Imperfect Parenting: Raising Children With Courage, Compassion, & Connection*. Audiobook. Boulder, CO: Sounds True, 2013.

Chua, Amy. *Battle Hymn of the Tiger Mother*. New York: Penguin Press, 2011.

Nathman, Avital Norman, ed. *The Good Mother Myth: Redefining Motherhood to Fit Reality*. Berkeley, CA: Seal Press, 2014.

O'Donnell, Liz. *Mogul, Mom, & Maid: The Balancing Act of the Modern Woman*. Brookline: Bibliomotion, 2014.

Senior, Jennifer. *All Joy and No Fun: The Paradox of Modern Parenthood*. New York: Ecco, 2014.

Slaughter, Anne-Marie. *Unfinished Business: Women, Men, Work, Family*. New York: Random House, 2015.

Valenti, Jessica. *Why Have Kids? A New Mom Explores the Truth About Parenting and Happiness*. New York: New Harvest, 2012.

Waugh, Daisy. *The Kids Will Be Fine: Guilt-Free Motherhood for Thoroughly Modern Women*. New York: Metropolitan Books, 2014.

Career

Adichie, Chimamanda Ngozi. *We Should All Be Feminists*. New York: Anchor Books, 2015.

Bock, Laszlo. *Work Rules! Insights From Inside Google That Will Transform How You Live and Lead*. New York: Twelve, 2015.

Brown, Brené. *Daring Greatly: How the Courage to Be Vulnerable Transforms the Way We Live, Love, Parent, and Lead*. New York: Gotham Books, 2012.

Collins, James C. *Built to Last: Successful Habits of Visionary Companies*. New York: HarperBusiness, 2002.

———. *Good to Great: Why Some Companies Make the Leap—and Others Don't*. New York: HarperBusiness, 2001.

———. *How the Mighty Fall: And Why Some Companies Never Give In*. New York: HarperCollins Publishers, 2009.

Drucker, Peter F. *Managing in the Next Society: Lessons from the Renown Thinker and Writer on Corporate Management*. New York: St. Martin's Press, 2003.

———. *The Effective Executive*. 50th Anniversary Edition. New York: HarperBusiness, 2017.

Gladwell, Malcolm. *David and Goliath: Underdogs, Misfits, and the Art of Battling Giants*. New York: Little, Brown & Co., 2013.

———. *Outliers: The Story of Success*. New York: Little, Brown & Co., 2008.

Hewlett, Sylvia Ann. *Executive Presence: The Missing Link Between Merit and Success*. New York: HarperBusiness, 2014.

Kay, Katty, and Claire Shipman. *The Confidence Code: The Science and Art of Self-Assurance—What Women Should Know*. New York: HarperCollins Publishers, 2014.

Kay, Katty, and Claire Shipman. *The Confidence Code for Girls: Taking Risks, Messing Up, & Becoming Your Amazingly Imperfect, Totally Powerful Self*. New York: HarperCollins Publishers, 2018.

Sandberg, Sheryl. *Lean In: Women, Work, and the Will to Lead*. New York: Alfred A. Knopf, 2013.

Shipman, Claire, and Katty Kay. *Womenomics: Write Your Own Rules for Success*. New York: HarperBusiness, 2014.

Spar, Debora L. *Wonder Women: Sex, Power, and the Quest for Perfection*. New York: Sarah Crichton Books, 2013.

Wolf, Alison. *The XX Factor: How the Rise of Working Women Has Created A Far Less Equal World*. New York: Crown Publishers, 2013.

ABOUT CLOENE DAVIS

In 1968, I graduated from Ouachita Baptist University with a Bachelor's degree in both Political Science and History. I fully expected to work in a public service career with politics in my future. But along the way, a series of opportunities presented themselves and I began to veer away from politics into Information Technology. All along the way, I have had to deal with gender bias.

I was a budget analyst in the Arkansas governor's office when they asked me to lead the development of an Information Strategy Plan for the State of Arkansas. My first thought was I did not know anything about computer programming. The powers that be saw it as an asset. They said I wouldn't have any preconceived ideas of what was important. They also told me I would get training for what I needed to know. Well, I have always been willing to accept a challenge, so I said yes.

My next big opportunity was at TWA implementing a new approach to software development called Information Engineering. This segued into leading the rewrite of the airline's Frequent Flyer Bonus (FFB) program using a brand new computer aided software engineering tool from Texas Instruments called the Information Engineering Facility (IEF). Both of these were high visibility and high risk. Once again, I found myself energized by the challenge.

The success of these projects (FFB was the first production-quality information system implemented using IEF) led to opportunities to explain how we did it at conferences sponsored by Texas Instruments.

The visibility I gained from this publicity was a big factor in my next big opportunity. I was hired by Sprint as a Senior Director to rebuild their Information Resource Management organization. When Sprint ventured into mobile communications, I was offered the job of Vice President of Information Resource Management at Sprint PCS. A couple of years later, the CIO at Sprint PCS asked me to move into the position of Vice President for Application Development, an organization that grew to 1,200 people.

When I left Sprint PCS, I worked as a consultant for a start-up company in San Jose. As that contract ended, I received a call from a former colleague asking if I would be interested in joining his team to help Disney launch a Disney-branded mobile phone as their Vice President of Technology. This was a very exciting opportunity and I jumped at the chance.

I spent the next few years as an account executive consultant managing teams of Information Technology consultants on projects for multiple telecommunications companies. I was very excited to have the opportunity to go to Dusseldorf, Germany to manage a consulting team for E-Plus.

All the while, I raised two children, whom I love dearly. I gave birth to my son near the beginning of my career at TWA, and then six years later, was blessed with the birth of my daughter. This was always part of my life's plan, "My Personal Passions." Today, my son and daughter are living their personal passions.

Made in the USA
Columbia, SC
30 April 2019